ESSAYS ON THE MORAL CONCEPTS

New Studies in Practical Philosophy
General Editor: W. D. Hudson

The point of view of this series is that
of contemporary analytical philosophy.
Each study will deal with an aspect of
moral philosophy. Particular attention
will be paid to the logic of moral discourse,
and the practical problems of morality.
The relationship between morality and
other 'universes of discourse', such as art
and science, will also be explored.

Published

R. W. Beardsmore *Art and Morality*
R. M. Hare *Practical Inferences*
R. M. Hare *Essays on Philosophical Method*
R. M. Hare *Essays on the Moral Concepts*
R. M. Hare *Applications of Moral Philosophy*
N. M. L. Nathan *The Concept of Justice*

Titles in preparation include
A. G. N. Flew *Crime or Disease?*
Pamela Huby *Plato and Modern Morality*
E. Kamenka *Freudianism and Ethics*
T. A. Roberts *The Concept of Benevolence*

ESSAYS ON THE MORAL CONCEPTS

R. M. HARE

White's Professor of Moral Philosophy
in the University of Oxford

MACMILLAN

First published 1972 by
THE MACMILLAN PRESS LTD
London and Basingstoke
Associated companies in New York Toronto
Dublin Melbourne Johannesburg and Madras

SBN 333 12926 1

Printed in Great Britain by
R. & R. CLARK LTD
Edinburgh

Contents

Acknowledgements

Proceedings of the Aristotelian Society, LV (1954-5); supp. vols XXV (1951), XXXVIII (1964). *Analysis*, XVII (1957). J. O. Urmson (ed.), *Encyclopedia of Western Philosophy and Philosophers* (Hutchinson, London, 1960). *Proceedings of the British Academy*, XLIX (1963).

Editor's Foreword

The present volume by Professor Hare contains papers most of which can be found scattered in learned journals but which the student will find it highly convenient to have now in one volume. Hare considers all these papers to be amongst his main contributions to ethical theory. They fill out the point of view presented in *The Language of Morals* and *Freedom and Reason*. The hitherto unpublished paper 'Wrongness and Harm' is Hare's latest contribution to the controversy between prescriptivists such as he and descriptivists such as Mr Warnock and Mrs Foot. This paper is particularly interesting because, as Hare himself says, it seeks to discover common ground between him and his opponents. The controversy between prescriptivists and descriptivists has been a focal point of interest in modern analytical philosophy, and all who study the subject seriously will need to take account of this paper.

University of Exeter   W. D. HUDSON

Preface

In this third volume of my collected papers I have included all but one of my main contributions, apart from my books *The Language of Morals* and *Freedom and Reason*, to the study of the moral concepts. The one that is omitted is 'The Promising Game' (*Rev. Int. de Philosophie*, LXX [1964]), which is available in two other volumes (*Theories of Ethics*, ed. P. Foot, and *The 'Is–Ought' Question*, ed. W. D. Hudson). They are for the most part controversial and even disputatious, as was inevitable in the climate in which they were written; I was concerned in them to distinguish my own position from, and to argue against, what I think to be serious and damaging errors in moral philosophy.

I have added a paper, written recently and now published for the first time, in which I try to sum up the present position in this field from my own point of view. It is unavoidably provisional and tentative. My own views are not static, and Mrs Foot and Mr Warnock, to mention but two with whom I have disagreed in the past, have important new contributions which are to appear shortly, and may even be out before this volume.[1] I thought it best, however, to try to see how much common ground I could find between my own views and theirs, as hitherto set out – for I am sure that there is more than might appear at first sight. The paper was read at a seminar on Utilitarianism given by Professor J. J. C. Smart and myself at Oxford in the autumn of 1970, and attended by a number of distinguished and able philosophers. To these, and especially to Professor Narveson and Mr Parfit, I owe a good shaking up of my ideas, of which the second half of this paper shows the still somewhat disordered fallout.

Details of first publication are given in the footnotes. Asterisks indicate footnotes added when reprinting in this volume. In the first volume of the set, *Practical Inferences*, I included a

[1] See below, p. 93 n.

bibliography of my published writings, in which the contents of the other volumes can be discovered. I have made a minimum of editorial corrections. I am grateful to the original publishers for giving their permission to reprint where necessary, and especially to the Aristotelian Society, to which three of these papers were originally delivered. I am also grateful to Dr Hudson, the editor of this series, for much kindness and help.

Corpus Christi College,   R. M. HARE
Oxford
1971

1   Freedom of the Will

Mr Hampshire has concentrated our attention on the problem, What is the import of the principle '"Ought" implies "can"' ? In order to dig still deeper into this problem, I shall adopt a somewhat different procedure from the first two speakers, and inquire what it is about the word 'ought' that gives rise to this principle; this will perhaps enable us to see more clearly what sort of 'can' it is that 'ought' implies. If this inquiry seems sometimes to take me rather far afield, my excuse is, that the confusions which have beset the problem of free will are so deep-seated, that nothing short of a closer understanding of the nature of moral language will dispel them.

1. '"Ought" implies "can"' not applicable only to moral 'ought'

Mr Hampshire argues that '"Ought" implies "can"' is an attempt to say, under what conditions a sentence may be said to express a moral judgement. That he says here 'moral', seems to indicate two things; one is that he accepts the traditional distinction between 'moral' and 'non-moral' uses or senses of the word 'ought' – a distinction which requires much more examination than it has recently received, though reasons of space compel me to leave it unexamined. The other is that, on the basis of this distinction, he regards the principle '"Ought" implies "can"' as peculiarly applicable to the moral use of 'ought' – so much so, that it enables us to distinguish moral judgements from other sorts of judgement. But in fact this principle does not apply only to moral uses of 'ought'; I am inclined to say that it applies to all uses of 'ought', or at any rate

The third paper of a Symposium with Professors Hampshire and Maclagan, reprinted by courtesy of the Editor from *Aristotelian Society Supp.*, xxv (1951). Part of §1, which is very similar to §10.3 of my *Language of Morals*, is omitted.

to all uses whose function it is to pass judgement of any kind upon actions or to give advice about them. Thus, for example, if I say 'They ought to make a bypass round the town', it is a perfectly good rebuttal of this advice or judgement to say 'But they can't; there's the sea on one side, and on the other the cliffs come so close that the cost would be prohibitive'. Similarly, if I say 'Smith ought to have tackled Robinson', it is a sufficient rebuttal to say, 'But he couldn't; he wasn't fast enough to catch him'. Or if I say 'They ought to make just one design of tank that would do equally well for support of infantry and for long-range penetration', those who disagree with me will be likely to seek to prove that it is impossible to design a tank that will do both these things satisfactorily.

We may take it, then, that ' "Ought" implies "can" ' is not a distinguishing mark of moral judgements as such; it is a distinguishing mark of a group of judgements of which moral judgements are one sub-group. We may characterise this group roughly by saying that it consists of those judgements whose function it is to do one of two things: either to give advice or guidance where there is a choice to be made, or to pass judgement upon a choice that has been made. . . . A general 'ought'-rule is a rule for answering questions of the form 'What shall I do ?' – a recipe for the production of particular pieces of advice. Singular 'ought'-sentences are means of instructing in, or instantiating, general 'ought'-rules. The whole of this linguistic structure loses its purpose in cases in which it is not or was not necessary to answer the question 'What shall I do ?' In such cases, the whole apparatus of advice, from its simplest forms to its most general, becomes irrelevant. You cannot instruct people in a rule to do the impossible. There is in this nothing peculiar to *moral* advice; if there are logical peculiarities which serve to distinguish moral advice or instruction from other sorts, they are to be sought elsewhere. 'Ought' implies 'can', whether in moral or non-moral contexts, because 'ought' is a prescriptive word.

2. *Advice and Persuasion, how different*

By saying that 'ought' is a prescriptive word, I may seem to have identified myself with a theory about the function of

moral judgements, from which in fact I dissent on a number
of fundamental points. It is a theory whose terminology Mr
Hampshire from time to time adopts, though I do not know
whether he agrees with it. Thus his determinist says:

> If it is established experimentally that moral exhortation
> and argument *have no effect whatever* upon certain types of
> conduct under certain conditions, then it is pointless to apply
> moral talk and argument to this type of conduct under these
> conditions,

and his libertarian says:

> From the fact that these [psychiatrical] forms of treatment
> are found to be more efficient in changing certain types of
> conduct, it does not follow that moral argument will make
> no difference at all and is utterly pointless in such cases (there
> may be a plurality of sufficient conditions of changing certain
> types of behaviour).

Thus both the antagonists seem to think that the function of
moral language is to 'have an effect on conduct' or to 'change
behaviour', and that in cases in which this function cannot be
fulfilled, it is pointless to use such language. I want to try to
show that, although moral talk is often used in order to bring
about changes in a person's behaviour, this is not the distinctive
function of such language, any more than it is the distinctive
function of a tennis racket to be used for measuring the height
of tennis nets, or for hitting one's victorious opponent over the
head.

In order to show this, I want to draw attention to two groups
of words for activities which differ from each other in respects
which are important for the study of the free will problem.
Such comparisons are bound to be loose, but this one seems to
me illuminating.

I: 'Advise', 'order', 'command', 'tell'.

II: 'Persuade', 'induce', 'cause', 'get'.

Here are some of the differences.

(1) Group I can be used performatorily, but Group II
cannot; thus I can say 'I advise you to make yourself scarce
before he comes', but not 'I persuade you to make yourself
scarce before he comes'. The reason for this peculiarity is as

follows: in order to advise, etc., all we have to do is to tell our
hearer something (say something to him); whatever he does
thereafter, he has had our advice or our orders. Therefore, to say
'I advise you . . .' is all that is required in order to advise, just
as to say, in due form, 'I promise . . .' is all that is required in
order to promise. Advising is a purely linguistic performance.
On the other hand, to say 'I persuade . . .' would not be all that
was required in order to persuade; to persuade, we have to
bring about an effect, a change in the hearer's behaviour; if we
do not bring about an effect, we have not persuaded him, and
bringing about an effect is not just talking, but something
further. The following comparison may elucidate this point:
we can say 'I (hereby) name this ship the Gargantua', but not
'I (hereby) push this ship into the water'; if I have said, in due
form, 'I name . . .', I have named; but if I have said 'I push . . .'
I have not thereby pushed; nor have I even tried thereby to
push; and similarly it will not do to say that to advise is to try
to persuade, or that words of the second group can be put in the
first simply by adding 'try to . . .'. I cannot say 'I try to persuade you . . .' any more than I can say 'I persuade you . . .'.

(2) For much the same sort of reason, Group II are what
have been called achievement words, whereas Group I are not.
I can say 'I advised him (or ordered him) to pick up his rifle,
but he wouldn't'; but 'persuaded' or 'induced' cannot be
substituted. It is self-contradictory to say 'I persuaded him, but
he wouldn't', just as it is self-contradictory to say 'I launched
the ship, but she stuck on the slipway and wouldn't go into the
water'. I have not launched her until she is in the water; and
I have not persuaded him to do it until he has done it, or at least
definitely resolved to do it. Moreover, he has to do it as a result
of my persuasion, and not from some other cause.

(3) Words of Group I refer to performances which have to be
some sort of communication by language; Group II is not so
restricted. Thus I can say 'We persuaded him to talk by using
the thumbscrew' or 'The presence of so many supporters induced him to speak frankly', but not 'We ordered him to talk
by using the thumbscrew' or 'The presence of so many supporters advised him to speak frankly'. In the thumbscrew case, we
see that a thumbscrew is not an instrument of communication
(contrast 'We ordered him to talk by using the heliograph');
it is one of coercion. Putting the thumbscrew on him does not

make him any the wiser, as flashing a heliograph at him from the other side of the valley may, what he is to do; he has to know what he is to do, before we can make him do it by torturing him. In the 'supporters' case, note that his supporters might advise him, but their presence does not. And it need not have been the presence of people that induced him; we might equally well say 'The presence of ten stout iron bars between him and his adversary induced him to speak frankly'; and here it is obvious that the iron bars do not *say* anything.

(4) I can say 'We persuaded him to talk by appealing to his baser (or better) nature' but not 'We advised him to talk by appealing to his baser (or better) nature'. If I may use an old-fashioned expression, advice is always addressed to a man *qua* rational being, whereas persuasion may be addressed to him *qua* affected by passions. Allied with this feature is the fact that we call advice or orders 'silly' or 'sensible', but persuasion or inducement 'effective' or 'ineffective'.

(5) If I am wondering what to do, I can say 'Please advise me, what I should do', or 'Give me your orders'; but it would be odd for me to say 'Please persuade me, what I should do': and if I said 'Give me some inducement', this would not be to ask what to do – it would be to seek, not an answer to a question, but something (as it were) to cause or help to cause me to put into practice one of the answers. Thus inducement and persuasion supply a different want from advice or orders or instructions; if I ask for the latter, I am asking what any free agent may ask of another without ceasing thereby to be a free agent; even in submitting to orders I am exercising my freedom (see below). But if I asked for the former, I should be asking for my freedom to be impaired in the sort of way in which propaganda, threats and bribes impair freedom.

(6) I might say, of a countersuggestible person, 'If you really want to get him to do it, tell him (or advise him) not to'; but I could not say 'If you really want to get him to do it, persuade him (or induce him) not to'; for this would be like saying 'If you really want to launch the ship, stop her going into the water'. Nor could I even say 'If you really want him to do it, try to persuade him not to'; the most I can say is 'If you really want him to do it, pretend to be (or act as if you were) trying to persuade him not to'. If I carried out this latter advice, I should only be pretending; I should not be really trying to

persuade him not to do it, but trying (by an unusual means) to persuade him to do it.

It seems to me that all these differences between the two groups of words are traceable to the same source; but I find myself unable to characterise this source more precisely than by saying that it has something to do with the freedom, as rational agent, of the person addressed. I want to make it clear, moreover, that I am not trying to suggest that advice resembles orders in any other ways than those to which I have drawn attention, nor that persuasion is exactly like inducement. There are of course further distinctions to be drawn, but they would not be relevant to my argument. The main distinction which I wish to make can perhaps be further elucidated by considering a parallel distinction in the sphere of factual assertions. We can persuade people of the truth of factual assertions, as well as persuading them to do things; and we can tell *that* as well as telling *to*. If I say 'I told him that the house was on fire', all I have claimed to have done is to communicate something to him in language, and left it to him to make up his own mind, whether what I have said is true. I have been successful in my undertaking if he has understood what I have told him – though of course, even if he has not understood, I have still told him. But if I say 'I persuaded him that the house was on fire', I claim to have done more than this; I claim to have made him believe (by fair means or foul) that the house was on fire. If we applied similar tests to those that I have applied in the previous case, we should in most, though not perhaps in all, cases (for nothing in philosophy is ever tidy) get similar results. This parallel seems to me to indicate, though I do not wish to press the point, that, though of course there is one division of the subject-matter according to which telling-to and persuading-to belong in one bag, and telling-that and persuading-that in another, there is also a different and just as important division according to which telling-to and telling-that belong in one bag, and persuading-to and persuading-that in another.

3. *Persuasion not the Distinctive Purpose of Moral Judgements*

Now we often hear it said that moral judgements have a prescriptive function; and I have already expressed a qualified adherence to this doctrine, which does bring out an important element in their meaning. But those who say this sort of thing have not always made it clear whether they are assimilating moral judgements to Group I or to Group II. To compare them with Group I is illuminating; but to assimilate them to Group II leads almost inevitably to some sort of ethical irrationalism. This is the source of the difficulty into which Professor Stevenson, for example, falls in *Ethics and Language*, ch. xi. There, having assimilated moral judgements to Group II, by saying 'A moralist is one who endeavours to influence attitudes', he finds it hard to make an adequate distinction between moralists and propagandists. But if we were able to show that moral judgements are more like Group I than Group II, we should be able to preserve this important distinction.

From the failure to make this distinction arises another doctrine of Stevenson's which has a direct bearing on the problem of free will. In ch. xiv of the same work, he commits himself to the view that 'ethics, although it *permits* complete determinism, *requires* only partial determinism' (p. 314). The view that ethics requires partial determinism is derived directly from the assimilation of moral judgements to Group II; for if it is the function of moral judgements to persuade, induce or influence, it is obvious that they would be pointless if such persuasion or inducement were unable to determine the agent's choice in any way. It is indeed true of *propaganda* that 'although it permits complete determinism, it requires only partial determinism'. But if moral judgements are like a kind of advice, not a means of persuasion, it is possible to restate the distinction between those circumstances in which they are relevant and those in which they are not, in a way which does not lead to such 'partial determinism'. Moral judgements are relevant to the same sort of situations (in respect of freedom of choice) as those to which advice or orders are relevant – namely, those where someone has to answer the question, 'What shall I do?' But advice or orders do not, as such, *determine*, even partially, the conduct of the person addressed. They only tell him what to do; they do not as such make him do it. For even orders do not impair the recipient's freedom to decide whether to obey them, any more than statements impair the hearer's freedom to decide whether to believe them.

It is true that, if the orders are coupled with implied threats or penalties for non-compliance, his freedom is impaired; he is under duress. But in this case it is the threats which impair his freedom, not the orders by themselves. Orders need not imply threats; suppose a devoted band of followers hanging on the lightest word of a leader; he says to them 'Go' and they go; but they are perfectly free not to go; they go because they have made up their minds to do his bidding. It is also true that parade-ground orders like 'Shun!' (which are a peripheral, not a typical example of the use of the imperative mood) causally affect the conduct of the fully-conditioned soldier. But it is not the fact that they are in the imperative mood that makes them have this effect, but the fact that he has been conditioned to react in a certain way – as most of us have not – to the hearing of these sounds. It would have been equally possible to train soldiers to react in the same way to the factual announcement (by the R.S.M.) 'The Colonel has come on —— parade'; and if this were done, we should not say that a sentence which was formerly in the indicative mood had been put into the imperative mood. The important point is, however, that even if we were to say that moral judgements are in some respects like orders, this would be a quite different thing from saying that their distinctive purpose is to induce, persuade, influence or in general causally affect the conduct of the person addressed.

We have to ask, then, whether moral judgements most resemble Group I or Group II. Let us admit to start with that moral judgements are very frequently used in order to persuade or induce, simply because one of the very best ways of getting someone to do something is often to tell him that it is the right, or a good, thing to do, or that he ought to do it. But this common use does not serve to distinguish moral judgements from other sorts of judgement. We may often persuade or induce someone to do something by making a factual assertion; for example, we may induce him to run out into the street by saying 'The house is on fire'. The truth is that almost any sort of utterance can on occasion be used in order to persuade; and therefore this function cannot be the distinguishing mark of moral utterance. In asking whether moral judgements most resemble Group I or Group II, we are not asking 'Can they be used for persuading?' but 'Is their distinctive purpose most like persuasion or advice?' Now that we have seen some of the respects in which advice is different from persuasion, we should be able to answer this question.

Activities of Group I are complete and have fulfilled their purpose when the hearer has understood what has been said; it is not requisite for the fulfilment of their purpose that he should thereby be caused to act on the advice or orders. This seems to me to be true of moral advice. Admittedly, if this is one of the occasions on which I am using a moral judgement in order to persuade, I do have this further intention, and my purpose is not fulfilled unless he acts on my advice. But there are many occasions on which I may advise morally without seeking to persuade, and if we attend to these, we see that moral advice is not necessarily persuasion, any more than factual assertion is persuasion because factual assertions are often used in order to persuade. For example, suppose I say to someone 'The right thing to do is to give him back the money', I might add 'I don't want to try to *persuade* you one way or the other – it's a matter on which you must make up your own mind without any exhortations from me – but since you ask me which I think is the right thing to do, I tell you that you ought to give him back the money'. Here I am deliberately refraining from influencing him; I am leaving him quite free to choose which course to take; but my moral advice does provide *guidance*. The difference is that between answering a question and giving a verbal shove. I do not want to be instrumental in *causing* him to suffer a financial loss, though I do both think and say that he ought of his own free will to submit to the loss. I do not want him subsequently to say to me 'If you had left me to make up my own mind, I should now be a richer man'.

If it were an essential purpose of moral judgements to persuade, they would become inappropriate in all cases where we knew that persuasion would be ineffective. But this is not the case. If a man is a very hardened offender, and if therefore the addressing of moral judgements to him will not alter his behaviour (whatever you say he is bound to go on doing it), we do not on that account stop saying that he ought not to act as he does. The reasons for this are worth examining. First, it might be suggested that, though there is no hope of persuading this individual to change his ways, our persuasion may be effective upon other people. The effect may be of two kinds. First, we may persuade other people to take up a certain moral attitude (namely of disapproval) towards him. But this explanation is obviously circular; for the problem remains, What would be the point of their taking up such an attitude? Secondly, we may persuade other people to avoid acting in the way that he does. In this explanation there is some truth; it is indeed true that 'He ought not to act as he does' invokes, and helps to teach, a general 'ought'-rule (see above). There might be some point in doing this, even if the man himself were known to be likely to take no notice, provided that other people learnt the lesson. So, if we substitute 'teach' or 'instruct in' for 'persuade', there is much to be said for this suggestion.

There is, however, still something wrong with it, as we can see if we compare this case with that of a man who is in a quite different sense bound to act as he does. Suppose a man is trespassing on my property, and I find out that he has unavoidably crashed in an aeroplane; I do not then say 'You ought to have kept off my property'. But according to the above explanation, I could say this; for I could indeed point to his action as an instance of breaking the general rule 'One ought to keep off other people's property': and by this means I might instruct other people in the rule. But, as I said above, you cannot instruct people in a rule to do the impossible. If other people can see that he could not have helped being on my property, the lesson becomes quite valueless; for to have value as a lesson, it would have to be an example of a general rule 'One ought not to act like this'. But 'One ought not to act like this' has obviously to be expanded in this case into 'One ought not to go-on-other-people's-property-when-one-can't-avoid-doing-so'; and this rule clearly cannot be taught.

Now why can we not say the same about the case of the hardened offender? Why does the fact that he isn't to be dissuaded, not make it impossible to use him as an instance for teaching the general rule? Should we not be able to say, here too, 'Nothing could teach the lesson that one ought not to go on acting as he does, when "go on acting as he does" means "go on acting in a way that one is bound to go on acting"'? But nevertheless we do say in this case, 'He ought not to go on acting as he does', although in the case of the airman we do not say 'He ought to have kept off my property'. And so there is clearly a difference between the two cases, though I find it difficult to put my finger on it.

We may perhaps suggest, in terms of the previous discussion, that the difference is that the hardened offender does, as the airman does not, have to answer, before doing the act, the question 'Shall I do this?', although the answer he gives to this question is bound to be always the same. Therefore his case can be used as an instance for teaching a general rule for answering like questions. The essential point of similarity between his case and that of people who are not hardened offenders is that both are in a position where they have to answer a question of the form 'What shall I do?'; and this makes moral rules applicable to both of them; for, as we have seen, a moral rule is one kind of rule for answering questions of this form.

This conclusion would not be altered if we had considered, not the case of a hardened offender, but that of one who, because of his heredity and environment, had never been, and never could have been, anything else but an offender. It is the case that we do say of such a person 'He ought not to act as he does', though we do not consider it sensible to scold him or try to persuade him, and have reasonable doubts about the morality of punishing him. We can say 'He ought not to act as he does' because he is, before he acts, in a position where he has to answer questions of the form 'What shall I do?'; that is, he satisfies one necessary condition for being what is usually called a moral agent, to whom moral judgements are applicable.

If the cases of the hardened and the 'born and bred' offender are different from that of the airman, what are we to say of that of the kleptomaniac? Is he more like the former or the latter? I admit that this is a borderline case which I still find perplexing, and which perhaps calls for a modification of our terminology. But at least it is clear that we do (and rightly) apply adverse moral judgements to the kleptomaniac; for we do not say 'Whereas ordinary people ought not to steal, it is quite all right for the kleptomaniac to do so'. On the contrary, we all agree that the kleptomaniac ought not to steal; for otherwise, there would be no reason for him to go to a psychiatrist in order to be cured of his kleptomania. It is true that we think it pointless to try to *persuade* him not to steal, and worse than pointless to *scold* him for stealing; but this is merely another indication that the function of moral judgements is different from that of persuading or scolding. It is precisely in instances like this that we see most clearly that, although 'ought'-sentences (including moral ones) are often used for scolding or persuasion (and often spoken in a scolding or persuasive tone of voice) this is not their distinctive purpose.

4. *Conclusion*

The considerations which I have advanced permit us to expose once for all a pernicious mistake about moral freedom which is more current that it ought to be. It is said that as prediction and causal explanation of human actions become easier and more widespread, moral language becomes in more and more cases unnecessary and pointless. But in fact, what becomes pointless, in certain cases, is a certain kind of attempt, by persuasion or scolding, to alter human behaviour. But the distinctive function of the word 'ought', in moral and non-moral contexts, is to instruct in or instantiate general rules for answering questions of the form 'What shall I do ?' It is a kind of general advice (§1). But advice is not the same sort of thing as persuasion (§2). Nor is it a distinctive function of moral judgements to persuade (§3). Therefore it does not follow from the fact that persuasion is found in a certain type of case to be pointless, that we have no further use for the word 'ought' in that type of case. So long as questions of the form 'What shall I do ?' continue to need answering, we shall have a use for general rules for answering them.

2 Universalisability

1. Since I planned this paper there has appeared in the Proceedings of the Society[1] a paper on very much the same subject by Mr E. A. Gellner. This sets out the issues so clearly that I have thought it best, instead of presenting the paper which I had planned, to continue the discussion where Mr Gellner leaves off. This will enable me to omit much tedious introductory matter which would otherwise have been necessary. I shall use much of Mr Gellner's terminology – not because I am entirely satisfied with its precision, but because I am myself unable to achieve any better compromise between brevity and rigour. My change of plan has made desirable a change of title, though the aim of my paper has not been substantially redirected. Like Mr Gellner, I must disclaim any intention of attempting accurate exegesis of Kant or of anyone else.

Gellner distinguishes between two types of valuation,[2] which he calls 'type E' and 'type U'. Of the former he says: 'Behaviour manifesting an E-type valuation cannot be universalised, i.e., its maxim cannot be deduced (in the sense in which an exemplification is deduced from the rule it exemplifies) from an open rule formulated with the help of only property-words and variables, but, of course, no proper names' (p. 161). Of U-type valuations he says that they are applications of 'a rule wholly devoid of any personal reference, a rule containing merely predicates (descriptions) and logical terms' (p. 163). Examples of the first kind of valuation, in addition to selfishness, are romantic love, loyalty and worship; of the second, according to Gellner, the impartial judgements of a judge.[3]

Reprinted by courtesy of the Editor from *Aristotelian Society*, LV (1954–5).

[1] *Ar. Soc.*, LV (1954–5) 157.

[2] I shall not discuss the terminological question whether E-type judgements can properly be called 'valuations'. See below, p. 16 n.

[3] This is, strictly speaking, inaccurate; for judges know that their jurisdiction is limited territorially or otherwise in ways which cannot be specified without the use of individual constants. This is one of the main

Other instances of U-type valuations are provided by at least some aesthetic judgements, and by judgements of logical validity. When we say that a poem is a good one, we are not appraising an individual in the ordinary sense. The Iliad is like the Union Jack ('by which I mean, not the tattered specimen the porter keeps in a drawer, but the flag designed in the nineteenth century').[1] Writing a poem for recitation on many occasions is like designing a flag for printing on many pieces of bunting. Both a poem, and a flag, and for that matter the property redness, are in *some* sense individuals (they can be referred to by singular terms); but none of them are individuals in any down-to-earth sense. And even if a poem is an individual, it is one which can be completely described by listing, in order, the words which it contains. If the poem, like that quoted by Plato in *Gorgias* 451e, consists itself entirely of U-type valuations, then no proper names, etc., will occur in this description even in mention, let alone in use. We do not even know the author of this poem. Thus at least some aesthetic judgements are U-type valuations; for if the object of a valuation can be specified without using proper names, etc., it is hard to see how these can be required for evaluating it.

Logical appraisals, however, provide an even clearer example. Consider the following judgement: 'The inference "If bats can fly, then some mammals can fly; but bats can fly; therefore some mammals can fly" is valid'. This judgement is an application of a rule (the *modus ponens*) which is clearly of type U. If any inference is valid, it must be valid in virtue of some *features* of the premisses and conclusion (whether these features are always formal or can be features of the content of the inference need not be here discussed). It must be possible in principle to state these features by means of a rule not containing proper names or anything else that would make it an

---

distinctions between legal and moral judgements. Gellner is prevented, by fear of begging the question which he is about to discuss, from giving moral judgements as an instance of what he *means* by 'U-type valuations'. Had he done so (as most of us would naturally do), he would not have been able to give his 'Existentialists' so long a run for their money.

[1] P. F. Strawson, *Ar. Soc.*, LIV (1953-4) 234. Strawson says that 'we should no doubt wish to include [the Union Jack] on the side of the general, as opposed to the particular . . . all these are things which we might well wish to classify with properties . . . or qualities . . . when we contrast these latter with individuals or particulars.'

E-type rule. If someone said 'The inference is valid just because Jones made it' or 'The inference is valid just because it was made at that particular moment' we should say that he did not understand the meaning of the word 'valid' as used by logicians.

2. I shall not assume, as does Gellner, that 'all actions are based on a rule or a maxim';[1] instead, I shall make the weaker claim that giving a *reason* for any action involves reference (explicit or implicit) to a rule, maxim or principle. This appears to me to be analytically true. For to give a reason for an action is first, to say something about the action, and secondly, to say or imply that this 'something about the action' is a reason for doing it. Now a reason cannot be a reason on just *this* occasion, and not on other similar occasions, any more than a rule of inference can apply in *this* case, but not in similar cases. I could not say, of the inference mentioned in the preceding paragraph, that the reason for its being valid is just a reason for *its* being valid, and not a reason for other inferences of the same form being valid. If there is some other case in which this is not a reason, there must be a difference between the cases to account for its not being a reason.

I do not claim, however, that a rule or maxim which is involved in giving a reason is always of type U. I am not presupposing, that is to say, the impossibility of giving reasons which involve maxims of type E, containing references to individuals. Thus 'It resulted in an improvement in Great Britain's balance of payments' might be given as a reason for an action by someone who would only think it a reason if it improved *Great Britain's* balance of payments, not if it improved the balance of payments of some other country, however similar qualitatively. In terms of the preceding paragraph, I do not claim that the 'something about the action' which is given as a reason cannot be something which involves reference to an individual, nor that 'similar cases' cannot be similar only in that they stand in similar relations to an individual. I cannot be accused, therefore, of making my thesis (that moral judgements, since reasons can be asked for them, are U-type valuations) analytic in virtue of the meaning of the word 'reason'; for I see no grounds in common language for confining the word 'reason'

[1] p. 158. This is verbally inconsistent with p. 164, last para., but there Gellner is speaking 'roughly', as is almost inevitable in the present stage of this controversy.

to reasons involving U-type rules.[1] I shall, however, argue later that it is analytic in virtue of the meaning of the word 'moral'.

Gellner says of U-type maxims that they must be able to be formulated 'with the help of a symbolism employing only predicates, individual *variables*, operators and logical connectives' (p. 164). It is important to see what is excluded and what permitted by this stipulation. Roughly speaking, proper names (in the ordinary, not the logical sense), personal pronouns (but not the pronoun 'one', nor the pronoun 'I' as it is used by some legal writers), and all token-reflexive expressions are excluded. A few examples will make these restrictions clear. The following maxims are of type U:

> One ought to keep one's promises.
> One ought to look after one's children.
> If I keep on my property a dangerous thing, I have
> a duty to prevent it from injuring my neighbours.

These are the sorts of maxims that we should be invoking, if, when asked for a reason why we did something, we said 'I promised to', or 'He's my son', or 'If I don't chain him up he'll go about biting all the neighbours'.

It must be noted that in all these cases the maxims are applicable in one sense to anyone, but in another sense only to one person. Only the person who has made the promise is bound to keep it; only the person who has begotten children is bound to look after them; only the person who keeps the dog is bound to prevent it from biting people. In each case of an application of these maxims, therefore, one person only is affected. But nevertheless the maxims apply to *anyone* who has promised, or who has begotten, or who keeps a dangerous thing.

It is easy, through confusion over this point, to take the restriction which governs admission of maxims to type U as being more restrictive than it really is. For example, there are certain kinds of patriotism which it excludes, and certain types which it does not. If a patriot thinks that he owes certain duties to his own country, but agrees that other people owe similar duties to their countries, his maxim is of type U ('one owes such and such duties to one's country'); the expression 'one's

---

[1] Some people might object to calling a judgement which contains a singular term a 'rule' or 'maxim'. I shall, however, use these words in the same wide sense as Gellner, and 'principle' likewise.

country' no more prevents this than do the expressions 'one's children' and 'one's promises'. But if he thinks that other people do not owe the same duties to their countries, then – unless he points to relevant differences between his country and others – his maxim is not of type U. Most of us, I hope, are patriots of the first kind. The thesis which I am maintaining in this paper (that moral judgements are U-type valuations) has, though analytic, great importance for questions of international morality, and is not, as might be thought, trivial; but I am here concerned merely to establish the thesis, not to show its importance.

It seems to me that Gellner has not sufficiently considered the distinction which I have just made. For on p. 160 he says 'Much will be made to hinge in this argument on the fact that certain classes of action and attitudes must include in their maxims such autobiographical, agent-mentioning clauses'. The example he gives is that of 'romantic love', in which, he says, the lover is bound to say that he would not love someone else exactly like his beloved; and in which, therefore, the only thing which distinguishes the beloved is primacy of encounter with the lover. To specify the attitude called 'romantic love', therefore, an 'agent-mentioning clause' is required, namely, that only one person is to be loved, and that persons similar to the loved person, but encountered by the lover after her, are not to be loved. To this it might be objected (1) that primacy of encounter is of no significance even in romantic love; a lover might equally well fall in love with the second or third of a set of identical persons, having passed over the first (just as sometimes someone falls in love with a person on the second occasion of their meeting, having been completely indifferent on the first occasion); and (2) that 'agent-mentioning clauses' do not prevent the attitude being of type U; for what makes us call Y 'X's beloved', and deny this title to Z, who is just like Y, is that X has done something to Y which he has not done to Z, namely, fallen in love with her. To say that one is to remain devoted to a person with whom one has fallen in love, but that one is not to accord the same devotion to others, though they may be just like her, is no more to utter an E-type maxim than to say that one is to do certain things for the person to whom one has made a promise, but is not necessarily to do them for others, though they may be just like this person. One cannot dance the waltz with two partners simultaneously; but instructions for dancing it do not need to contain proper names. It would appear that Gellner's confusion, at the beginning of his paper, of 'agent-mentioning clauses' in the sense of 'clauses containing bound individual *variables*' and 'agent-mentioning clauses' in the sense of 'clauses containing individual constants' enables him to give much greater plausibility to the 'Existentialist' thesis than it would have, were this distinction observed. This is a lapse on his part; for on p. 165 (top) he shows himself well aware of this distinction, by putting the word 'variables' (as I have done above) into italics.

3. There is, however, an even more important error in Gellner's presentation of the 'Existentialist' case – an error for which Kant is perhaps to blame. Gellner rightly distinguishes, on pp. 164–5, between first-order rules 'that can be formulated with the help of a symbolism employing only predicates, individual *variables*, operators and logical connectives', and the second-order rule which states the requirement that all our first-order rules should be of this sort; this second-order rule, Gellner says, 'employs, in addition to the items mentioned above, only predicate *variables* instead of actual predicates'. But later, in his criticism of 'Kantianism', Gellner seems to me to fail to observe the distinction between these two kinds of rule. It is only thus that he is led to say that '*no* actual valuation ... *could* fit the rigour of pure formality (be completely of type U)' and that 'to some extent at least all our valuations are of type E' (p. 175). The second-order rule is purely formal, because it contains (or mentions) only predicate variables. But the first-order rules (which correspond to Kant's 'maxims') are not formal in the least; they contain material predicates such as 'tell lies' or 'neglect one's natural gifts'. Nor is there any reason (whatever Kant's preferences may have been) why a first-order rule should not be of any desired degree of specificity, without infringing the second-order rule. Thus 'One ought not to tell lies unless this is necessary in order to save innocent lives' is just as much a U-type maxim as 'One ought not to tell lies'. Universality, in the sense in which U-type maxims are universal, is not a matter of degree; to suppose that it is, is to confuse the term 'universal' (as opposed to 'singular') with the term 'general' (as opposed to 'specific'). I shall have more to say later about this confusion.

It is not therefore necessary, if a maxim is to be of type U, that it should 'fit the rigour of pure formality'. Those who have supposed it necessary have done so chiefly because (following one possible interpretation of Kant's obscure reasoning) they have insisted on the first-order rules being *deducible* from the second-order rule. Gellner's 'Existentialists' say (p. 175) that choice 'cannot or should not be deduced from a formal, and consequently blessedly non-arbitrary rule such as the one Kant hoped for'. But we can happily agree with this statement without being Existentialists; for the relation of the first-order rules to the second-order rule (and *a fortiori* that of actual choices to the second-order rule) is not that of deduction, nor anything like it. If it were, the first-order rules would have to be as formal as the second-order rule; and then it would indeed be true that 'no actual specific valuation was entailed in the formal moral principle' (p. 175).

The desire to treat the first-order rules as deducible from the second-order rule arises from the oldest and most ineradicable vice of moralists – the unwillingness to make moral decisions. If we could establish a formal, *a priori* (and yet somehow synthetic) principle, and then deduce maxims from it to govern all our conduct, we should have succeeded in finding a set of moral principles to guide our lives without making up our own minds about a single moral question. Whether Kant thought this possible I do not know; on the one hand, he gives ample excuse for such an interpretation; but on the other to interpret him in this way is to make him guilty of basing his morality on what he calls Heteronomy of the Will. However that may be, a correct statement of the relation between the second-order and first-order principles can be made in Kantian language, even if Kant himself would not have agreed with it. The second-order principle analyses the concept 'rational principle' (in that sense of the expression in which it means 'U-type maxim'). I shall contend later that it is part of the meaning of the word 'moral' that moral principles are rational in this sense. A person who accepts this second-order principle has not thereby had all his moral problems solved for him; he has to do something further in order to obtain his first-order maxims, namely, exercise his autonomous, rational will by 'making laws for himself' which are of the form prescribed by the second-order principle, but are not themselves formal. In simpler language, the first-order principles are not deduced from the second-order principle; they are framed in accordance with it. Kant may have thought that there was only one set of first-order principles that could be framed in accordance with the second-order principle; but in this he was wrong. There is an infinite variety of possible first-order principles; to decide between these is our job as autonomous rational agents.

There are two objections which a 'Kantian' might make at this point:

(1) *You are making our choice between first-order principles a matter of mere 'inclination'.*[1] This objection leaves me quite unmoved. We are choosing between these principles. No doubt we have the sort of principles we have because we are the sort of people that we are. The 'because' here is logical; it signifies an entailment in the strictest sense; but it is very important not to be mistaken about the nature of this entailment. It is not that we can deduce statements of the form 'I ought always to, etc.', from statements describing what sort of person I am. This would be to offend against Hume's Law.[2] It is rather that to have moral principles of a certain kind *is* to be a certain kind of person. I could not, therefore (since I am *this* kind of person), have different moral principles from those which I actually have; but neither can I set about choosing between moral principles by first asking what sort of person I am and then deducing the correct principles from premisses giving this information. If I am trying to decide what my ultimate moral principles are to be, I cannot deduce the answer from anything whatever. To this extent the 'Existentialists' are right, and analytically so, in virtue of the meaning of the word 'ultimate'. But to say that ultimate moral principles cannot be deduced from other principles is not to say that they are not themselves principles.

(2) *You are making our choice between first-order principles 'arbitrary'.* This objection also leaves me unmoved; for it rests on a simple confusion about the meaning of the word 'arbitrary'. I think it wrong to torture people; but I can give no ulterior reason for this (no reason, that is to say, which does not merely repeat in other words that torturing people is wrong). I think

[1] Cf. Gellner, p. 174.
[2] *Treatise*, III i i, last para.

it wrong to torture people, because of what torturing is.
Suppose now that our objector says 'In that case, since you can
give no reason for thinking that torture is wrong, other than
that it is torture, is not your decision to accept this principle
arbitrary ?' Shall I not answer, 'Yes, in the sense that I accept it
libero arbitrio (I was perfectly free to adopt instead the principle
that torture is morally permissible); but not in the sense that it
does not matter which principle I accept (have I not, in saying
that torture is wrong, said that it *does* matter ?)' ? One might
as well say that my choice between being myself tortured and
being given a glass of beer is arbitrary, because no reason can
be given for it other than that torture is what it is, and glasses
of beer what they are. Yet, in a sense, I choose *libero arbitrio*
between beer and the thumbscrew.

4. The position of my argument so far may be summed up
as follows: (1) All actions for which there are reasons involve
maxims. (2) These maxims may be either of type E or of type U.
(3) Certain arguments, which have been used to show that all
actual valuations are of type E, are based on confusions. I
now wish to argue that all *moral* valuations are of type U –
or, which comes to the same thing, that whenever moral
reasons are given for actions, the maxims involved are of type
U. I shall conclude by considering further objections to this
view.

That all moral uses of the word 'ought' involve a U-type
maxim is apparent, if we consider the following imaginary
conversation between a 'Kantian' and an 'Existentialist':

E.: You oughtn't to do that.
K.: So you think that one oughtn't to do that kind of thing ?
E.: I think nothing of the kind; I say only that *you* oughtn't
to do *that*.
K.: Don't you even imply that a person like me in circum-
stances of this kind oughtn't to do that kind of thing
when the other people involved are the sort of people
that they are ?
E.: No; I say only that *you* oughtn't to do *that*.
K.: Are you making a moral judgement ?
E.: Yes.
K.: In that case I fail to understand your use of the word
'moral'.

Most of us would be as baffled as the 'Kantian'; and indeed we should be hard put to it to think of *any* use of the word 'ought', moral or non-moral, in which the 'Existentialist's' remarks would be comprehensible. Had the 'Existentialist' said 'Don't do that', instead of 'You oughtn't to do that', the objections of the 'Kantian' could not have been made; this illustrates one of the main differences between 'ought' and ordinary imperatives. Indeed, the fault of the 'Existentialists' might be characterised thus: because moral judgements are like ordinary imperatives in some respects, they conclude that they are like in all respects.[1]

A less truculent 'Existentialist' might agree with the 'Kantian's' first remark, but seek to introduce singular terms at a later stage, taking advantage of a loophole which I mentioned above (§2). He might say that, although he does indeed think that one oughtn't to do that kind of thing, he is including in 'that kind of thing' only acts which cause Great Britain's balance of payments to deteriorate. In that case, the 'Kantian' will ask, 'So you think that a person like me, standing in this kind of relation to a country like Great Britain, oughtn't to cause its balance of payments to deteriorate?' If the 'Existentialist' refuses to make this step, the result of the argument will be the same as before. I shall in what follows consider the first and simpler of these two arguments; all that I shall say could be extended to fit the more elaborate one.

The judgement 'A person like me in circumstances of this kind oughtn't to do that kind of thing when the other people involved are the sort of people that they are' is not, it is true, of type U. It contains the token-reflexive expressions 'me', 'this', 'that', and 'they'. But, nevertheless, all these expressions occur in the context of words attributing *similarity;* the judgement says 'people like me'; 'circumstances of this kind'; 'that kind of thing'; and 'the sort of people that they are'. Now the expression 'like *a*', where '*a*' is an individual constant, is of such a character that it is hard to call it in the strict sense either a universal or a singular term. It is not, *prima facie*, universal, since it contains a reference to an individual; it is not singular, because it defines an open class. 'Like' is, of course, the name of a relation (a two-place predicate); and 'like *a*' is what used to be called a relational

---

[1] This point was discussed more fully in my *Language of Morals* (*LM*), pp. 155, 175.

property. But this does not help us to say whether maxims containing it are of type E or type U. With most other two-place predicates, my inclination would be to say that their occurrence with individual constants in a maxim would make it of type E. But with 'like' I do not feel this inclination. It might be argued that 'like a' is best treated, in spite of appearances, as a universal term. A person who argued thus would first point out that *all* such universal terms as are ostensively definable are definable by means of expressions of the form 'like x' and 'unlike y'. Thus the universal expression 'one metre long' is defined in terms of the expression 'like m (in length)' – where 'm' is an individual constant, the name of the platinum rod in Paris. In the same way the universal term 'red' would be defined (if we had to define it) in some such terms as 'like r_1 but unlike s_1, like r_2 but unlike s_2, etc.' – where 'r_1', 'r_2', etc., are the names of, or definite descriptions of, red objects; 's_1', 's_2', etc., the names of, or definite descriptions of, objects which are not red; and the object r_1 is like the object s_1 in nearly all other respects, and so on. Therefore, unless we admit that 'like a' is a universal term, we shall have to admit that universal terms are equivalent to terms which are not universal; and this is absurd.

It is not necessary for my argument, however, to make so extreme a claim; and since I have doubts about the use of the word 'equivalent' in the above reasoning, I shall not make it. All I need to claim is that, wherever the expression 'like a' is used in a maxim, it must be possible in principle to substitute a universal term for this expression without altering the import of the maxim. This universal term may not already exist in our language; but if necessary we can coin a new universal term for the purpose. The possibility of doing this shows that, if we have established that a man who makes a moral judgement containing the word 'ought' must agree to a maxim in which all individual constants are preceded by the word 'like' or its equivalent, then we have also established that a man who makes such a judgement must agree to some U-type principle. For by performing the above substitution we have finally eliminated the individual constants from his maxim.

It is important, however, to notice the difficulty which is concealed by the words 'in principle' in the preceding paragraph. I said that, if there were no suitable universal term in our language, we could coin one. But in order to coin a word we have not only to choose a sound, but to give it a meaning. The new term that we are going to coin is to mean the same as 'like a'. But, as is well known, the expression 'like a' is an incomplete symbol; if anyone uses it, he is liable to be asked 'like a in what respect?' Unless we are able to answer this question, we shall have, in saying that our new universal term means 'like a', given it no definite meaning.

This difficulty has sometimes been expressed by saying that, even if there is a principle or maxim involved in every moral judgement, it is seldom possible to *formulate* this principle or maxim. We thus reach the apparently unsatisfactory position that, while to deny that *any* principle is involved is to invite incomprehension, to ask *what* principle is involved, if a precise answer is demanded, is to make an unreasonable request. But it is not hard to show that this difficulty is more apparent than real. We saw above that *all* universal terms which are ostensively definable must be reducible to this same unsatisfactory formulation 'like x'. By means of such formulations, we can explain the meaning of 'red' with any required degree of precision; but we cannot render it precise beyond possibility of doubt. Neither 'red' nor many other empirical predicates in our language have a sufficiently exact use for us to be able to do this. I see no reason for demanding a kind of precision in the formulation of moral principles which we know to be impossible in formulating the meanings of the bulk of the predicates in our language; indeed, since the moral principles would have to be formulated in terms of these same inexact predicates, the task would be Sisyphean. But there is nothing in all this to dishearten those who think that all moral judgements involve principles. When we consider the degree of precision which lawyers, who are subject to just the same disabilities, achieve in formulating the principles involved in legal decisions, we shall be inclined to say what they say – *de minimis non curat*. We can be as precise as we wish, or as we need.

This analogy between the languages of factual description, of law and of morals is not accidental. It arises from the fact that the moral words normally have a descriptive meaning in addition to their evaluative meaning; so far as their descriptive meaning goes, they behave very like descriptive words; and they have descriptive meaning only because judgements in which they are used involve principles.[1]

Very often, instead of the improbable dialogue which I set out above, we have conversations of the following kind:

A.: You oughtn't to do that.
B.: So you think that one oughtn't to do that kind of thing?
A.: Yes; it would be dishonest (or cruel, or vulgar).

Here *A* is not merely admitting that there is a principle involved, but going some way towards saying what this principle is. There is a class of value-words whose evaluative meaning is secondary to a very definite descriptive meaning.[2] We can say 'too honest' almost without paradox. 'Dishonest', though still evaluative (a dispute about whether it would be dishonest to do a certain thing would still be a moral dispute) has as definite a descriptive meaning as many purely descriptive words. Thus its use *specifies* a principle which was left unspecified by the more general 'you oughtn't'. But by saying 'dishonest' *A* does not go the whole way, or even as far as it is reasonable to ask, towards a complete specification of his principle; *B* might well go on 'What is dishonest about it?', and get an answer. But a complete specification is unattainable.

Both in deciding to apply a descriptive predicate, and in deciding that we ought to do some particular thing, we make this decision in the light of certain salient features of the situation as we see it, without bothering about how we would use the predicate, or apply the moral principle, in certain hypothetical, borderline, obscure or improbable cases. This is partly because we do not have the leisure, unless we are professional casuists, to consider these cases, and partly because it is not desirable to commit ourselves in advance about what we would say in a peculiar situation. Just as judges on the whole confine their remarks to the case before them and to cases which *have* occurred, and do not speculate about odd cases which might arise, until they actually do arise; and just as a scientist might not like being asked what he would say if he discovered some substance like phosphorus in other respects but which melted at an unusual temperature,[3] but would wait until such

[1] Cf. *LM*, pp. 132, 134.
[2] Cf. *LM*, p. 121.
[3] Cf. *LM*, p. 167, and G. H. von Wright, *Logical Problem of Induction*, ch. iii.

a disturbing substance was actually discovered; so we, as moralists, normally consider actual cases and thus leave our principles open – though at the same time determinate enough, like the language of the scientist and the precedents of the lawyers, to provide guidance in such cases as we think likely to arise. We steer a middle course between the hidebound inflexibility of the man who knows what he ought to do in a new situation even before he has properly considered its special features, and the neurotic indetermination of the man who cannot ever make up his mind what he ought to do, even in comparatively familiar situations, because he is never satisfied that he has exhausted their infinite particularity. The latter can learn nothing from experience; the former stops learning too early.

5. There is one further objection to my thesis which must be considered – though not at length, for it rests on two ancient confusions which have been sufficiently often exposed. The first of these confusions is that of supposing that, since a name can never be logically equivalent to a description, what can be named (the individual) can never be described. This confusion is pecularly attractive to those who do not themselves like being described, especially by scientists and moralists. They have thus been led to say that *people*, and the situations in which people find themselves, are 'unutterably particular', and thus beyond the reach of any universal predicate or principle. Examples of this view are to be found in Mr Mayo's *The Logic of Personality* (p. 28) and in the utterances of the pseudonymous philosopher in the dialogue which forms the centrepiece of Miss Murdoch's delightful novel *Under the Net*. But in fact individuals can be described as fully and precisely as we wish by the ingenious device (which is even older than the confusion of these philosophers) of putting the names of the individuals as subjects and appending predicates to them.

It is odd that Existentialists, who are especially prone to make this confusion, also tend to think novel-writing a superior way of discussing moral questions compared with their discussion in terms of principles. Odd, because no work of fiction can be about a concrete individual. If, after reading *Under the Net*, I have formed a certain moral opinion about its hero, my opinion is not, and cannot be, an opinion about a unique

individual, because there is, literally, no such individual. I have
formed an opinion about a *type* of individual – a type which has
been very skilfully and minutely specified. Thus my opinion
not only *involves* a type U principle; it *is* one. I think that about
anyone like Jake a certain judgement should be made. *How* like
Jake an actual person has go to be, before I judge him similarly,
is, of course, a question which may not (though it may) trouble
me. But in the case of judgements about fictional characters the
Existentialist thesis does not even have the initial plausibility
which it has in the case of judgements about real characters.
For in the latter case we can at least deceive the undiscerning
by saying 'My judgement is about *this* concrete existing
individual whom you see (of whom you are *aware*, as Mr Mayo
would put it); and it would not necessarily apply to anyone
else, however like him'. But of a fictional character we cannot
be *aware* in this mystical sense; we can only have him *described*
to us in greater or less detail.

   At the root of this first confusion lies a second one, to which
I have already alluded – that between the words 'general' (in
the sense in which it is the opposite of 'specific') and 'universal'
(as contrasted with 'singular' and 'particular' – the latter itself
an ambiguous term). I do not wish to maintain that it is incorrect to use either of these terms in a variety of different ways,
some of which overlap, but only that there is an important distinction to be made. If we do not make it, we shall be taken in
by the argument that, since people and situations are very
complex entities, and since, therefore, descriptions of them will
need to be highly *specific*, it follows that no description in
universal terms can be given of them, and therefore no *universal*
principle propounded about them. If 'general' were substituted
for 'universal' in this argument, it would be valid; it is indeed
impossible to propound moral (or for that matter psychological)
principles which have both a high degree of generality and a
high degree of precision. We can speak generally if we are content to speak loosely and to admit the possibility of exceptions;
but of matters which are complex and various we cannot be
both general and precise. But we can make universal statements
which are as precise as we please (there is no such thing as
complete precision). The introduction of uneliminable singular
terms in order to deal with the complexity of the subject-matter
(which is what these philosophers evidently wish to propose) is

both unnecessary and unhelpful; to speak, we require both subjects (singular) and predicates (universal); and, even if there were any difficulty in using these instruments, a recommendation to silence would not *solve* it.

3 Geach: Good and Evil

Mr Geach has suggested to me that I publish a reply to his article on Good and Evil.[1] From this I conclude that he regards me as a constituent part of the composite Aunt Sally which he calls 'The Oxford Moralists'. I am not, however, concerned to defend this heterogeneous monster. In the stage-battle which Geach has with his creature I find myself engaged on both sides; for although some of the views of 'The Oxford Moralists' are more or less recognisable versions of mine, so also are a good many of Geach's own arguments and in some cases examples.* Neither am I going to attack his main thesis that 'good' is an attributive adjective, since I agree with it.[2]

How composite a creature Geach's Aunt Sally is, may be seen by considering a typical paragraph of his paper – the third complete paragraph on p. 36. There 'The Oxford Moralists' are said to hold the following positions:

(1) The function of 'good' is primarily not descriptive at all but commendatory.

Reprinted from *Analysis*, XVII (1957). Paras. 2 and 3 incorporate small amendments made to conform to alterations in Geach's text when both papers were reprinted in *Theories of Ethics*, ed. P. Foot.

[1] *Analysis*, XVII 2 (1957) 33–42. I wish to thank Mr Geach for his kindness in lending me the full typescript of a longer paper of which his published article forms the opening section; and also for elucidating, in correspondence, the meaning which he attaches to the word *ratio*, and the use to which he wishes to put this concept in his theory.

* In saying this, I was not censuring Geach (for in philosophy arguments and examples are common property), but rather raising a doubt as to what his target could be.

[3] This thesis has been common form among Oxford moralists for many years; so far as I remember, it first entered my own mind when discussing Frege with Professor Austin. In *Foundations of Arithemetic* (ed. and tr. Austin, pp. 28 ff.) Frege, following a suggestion of Baumann, points out that cardinal numbers are, in Geach's sense, attributive. But some acknowledgement is also due to Joseph and ultimately to Aristotle, *Eth. Nic.*, 1 6. The thesis, without the terminology, is to be found in my *Language of Morals* (*LM*), p. 133.

(2) 'That is a good book' means something like 'I recommend that book'.

(3) 'That is a good book' means something like 'Choose that book'.

It may be that Geach has not noticed the difference between commending and recommending,[1] or between either of them and the various purposes for which the imperative is used; or between any of these various things and the two different things which are expressed by the sentences 'What a wonderful wicket Hutton was batting on' and 'May you have such a wicket when you bat', which he manages to cram into this mixed bag. That the last example comes from *LM*, p. 118, makes it look as if, according to that book, the commendatory meaning of 'good' is to be identified with the expression of exclamations or wishes. But this view does not occur in the text of the book. If Geach wishes to attribute these confusions to others besides himself, ought they not to be named?[2]

It is not clear to me, either, why it should be thought that 'Oxford Moralists', when confronted with the 'good wicket' example, would use the argument which Geach puts in their mouths. The example is given by Geach as a case where 'the force of "good" is purely descriptive'. 'Oxford Moralists' would answer, says Geach, 'that here "good" is used in quotation marks; Hutton was batting on a "good" wicket, i.e. a wicket such as cricket fans would call "good", i.e. would commend and choose'. Now there are indeed cases in which 'good' is used in this 'inverted-commas' way;[3] but this is not one of them. Those are cases where the word 'good' has no evaluative meaning, because the speaker is not himself com-

---

[1] According to the O.E.D. 'commend' is sometimes used with the sense 'recommend'; but this use is not common, and it is not in this sense that the word occurs in *LM*. We normally use 'recommend' when a *particular* choice is in question, but 'commend' when a thing is being mentioned as in general 'worthy of acceptance or approval'.

[2] I myself claim no property in any of these positions attributed to 'The Oxford Moralists'. My view is that 'good' has, normally, both descriptive and evaluative (commendatory) meaning, and that the evaluative meaning is primary. This position is to be distinguished from (1) above, in which the words 'at all' *seem* to imply that the word has 'primarily' (whatever that means) no meaning at all but commendation; and this latter position I specifically reject in *LM*, pp. 121 f.

[3] See *LM*, p. 124.

mending, but only alluding to the commendation of some other (normally well-known) set of people. But in the present case the writer is certainly commending the wicket (though he is not doing some of the other things which Geach confuses with commending). In this context, no doubt, the primary purpose of saying, in a newspaper report, that it was a good wicket is 'to inform readers what description of wicket it was';[1] but it can surely be supposed that the writer and most of his readers are themselves cricket-fans and therefore accept the standard of commendation which is attached to the phrase. If this standard of commendation were not, by common use, attached to the phrase, it could not be used, as it is here, for giving information. Moreover, Geach's reasoning depends on the assumption that you can prove the meaning of an expression to be not primarily evaluative by adducing *one* context in which it is used with a primarily descriptive purpose. There could scarcely be a weaker argument. It is strange, too, that Geach should think that someone who fully understood the game could 'supply a purely descriptive sense for the phrase "good batting wicket" regardless of the tastes of cricket-fans'. Would he say that the standards according to which this phrase is applied to wickets have nothing to do with the preferences of batsmen ?

Another instance of confusion in the minds of 'The Oxford Moralists' is to be found in the immediately succeeding passage. They evidently do not distinguish between saying that to call a thing a good A is to *guide* choice and saying that it is to *influence* or *affect* choice. To commend may be to seek to guide choice; but it certainly is not necessarily to seek to influence or affect choice.[2] It is not (as Geach might put it) part of the *ratio* of the word 'good', or of the word 'commend', or even of imperatives,

---

[1] See *LM*, p. 118.

[2] I have tried to make this distinction clear in my articles 'Imperative Sentences', *Mind*, LVIII (1949), reprinted in my *Practical Inferences*, pp. 19 ff.; and 'Freedom of the Will', pp. 1–12 of this volume; and in *LM*, pp. 13–16. Similar distinctions are made by Dr Falk, 'Goading and Guiding', *Mind*, LXII (1953), p. 145, and by Professor Cross, 'The Emotive Theory of Ethics', *Ar. Soc. Supp.*, XXII (1948), esp. pp. 139 f.; but Cross does not deal with the matter very fully, and Falk seems to me to put imperatives on the wrong side of the divide. Perhaps the matter will become clearer if and when Professor Austin puts something in print about his general distinction between illocutionary and perlocutionary force (that is to say, between what we are doing *in* saying '*p*' and what we are trying to do *by* saying '*p*').

that 'good'-sentences or commendations or imperatives have a causal influence on our behaviour. Against such a theory Geach's 'ants in your pants' example provides an objection, though one which is not by itself conclusive. It is, indeed, a vulgarised version of an example which I myself used, in the first of the articles referred to, to show this in the case of imperatives: 'If you want a man to take off his trousers, you will more readily succeed by saying "A scorpion has just crawled up your trouser-leg" than by saying "Take off your trousers"'. Some philosophers, such as that distinguished Cambridge and Ann Arbor moralist Professor Stevenson, have held that both moral judgements and imperatives are, *de ratione*, action-affecting; others, like Dr Falk, have held that imperatives are, but moral judgements not. It is certainly objectionable to say that moral judgements are; and in this I agree with Geach. But, again, if he thinks that this objectionable view is current in Oxford, should not its holders be identified by name?

In short, to be a prescriptivist (which is perhaps the best name for what I am) is not necessarily to be an emotivist of any kind; and in particular, it is not to be an emotivist of the kind which confuses moral judgements with propaganda. Perhaps, if Geach reflects on this distinction, 'commending' will in future cause him no greater discomfort than 'good' itself does. For, once this misunderstanding is cleared away, the chief reason is removed for doubting what the *O.E.D.* says about 'good'. The very first thing which this dictionary says about the meaning of 'good' is that it is 'the most general adjective of commendation'. The fact that this definition is quoted without dissent by Sir David Ross (than whom nobody could be a stauncher descriptivist) strengthens the link between 'good' and commending;[1] and it really becomes very hard to deny this association when we consider what the same dictionary says about the word 'commend'. This it defines as 'To mention as worthy of acceptance or approval'; 'approve' is defined as 'to pronounce to be good, commend'. Putting these two definitions together we get: 'Commend: to mention as worthy of ... being pronounced to be good', or, for short, 'to mention as being good'. If this is what 'commend' means, how can it be as improper as Geach evidently thinks it is to say that 'good' has as its primary function to commend?

[1] See *The Right and the Good*, p. 66.

It might at this point be objected that, although the dictionary is quite right to connect 'good' with 'commend' in the way that it does, I am wrong to take the further step of connecting commending with the guidance of choices. This objection might be made by someone who wished at all costs to keep 'good' a purely descriptive word, in spite of its connection (which can hardly be denied) with commending. But this argument is not open to Geach; for on pp. 38f. of his paper he says 'It belongs to the *ratio* of "want", "choose", "good" and "bad", that, normally, and other things being equal, a man who wants an A will . . . choose an A that he thinks good and will not choose an A that he thinks bad'. Geach is no doubt right to say that the doctrine *quidquid appetitur, appetitur sub specie boni* is not as it stands analytic, 'since the qualifying phrase "normally and other things being equal" is necessary for the truth of this statement'. But if this qualifying phrase is added to the statement, it becomes, not merely true, but analytically so; and this is all that is required in order to show that the meaning of the word 'good' is *not* purely descriptive.

My principal purpose in this article, to which I now turn, is to appraise Geach's own suggestion as to how the word 'good' has descriptive force. That it *has* descriptive force I have said many times; but Geach wants to go further. Whereas I maintain that the meaning which is common to all instances of the word's use cannot be descriptive, and that this common meaning is to be sought in the evaluative (commendatory) function of the word, Geach maintains that this common meaning is a kind of descriptive meaning. Thus, he thinks, 'good' has the same descriptive meaning in the expressions 'good knife' and 'good stomach' although, as he and I agree, 'the traits for which a thing is called "good" are different according to the kind of thing in question' (p. 37). He thinks that this can be so because, although there are no common traits, the meaning of the word 'good', taken in conjunction with that of the word 'knife' or that of the word 'stomach', enables us to specify the traits which things of these kinds have to have in order to be called 'good'. He compares this with the way in which, though we do not have to multiply 2 by the same factor, in order to get its square, as we do 3 in order to get *its* square, nevertheless the expression 'the square of' has a common meaning; given a number, its square is determinate.[1]

I was aware of this possible line of argument when I wrote *LM*, pp. 99–103; and that passage contains the considerations which in my view provide an answer to it. There is a certain class of words (called in *LM* 'functional words') for which this manœuvre is very inviting. 'A word is a functional word if, in order to explain its meaning fully, we have to say what the object it refers to is *for*, or what it is supposed to do'.[2] Examples of functional words are 'auger', 'knife' and 'hygrometer'. The dictionary definitions of all these words include a reference to the functions of objects so called. Therefore, if we know the meaning of 'good', and also that of 'hygrometer', we are in the way of knowing what traits a hygrometer has to have in order to be called a good one (indeed, we know very well one of the traits which would entitle us to call it a bad one, viz., habitually registering as the moisture-content of a gas a different moisture-content from that actually possessed by the gas).

Where 'good' precedes a functional word, most of what Geach says is correct. He passes uncritically, however, from this truth about functional words to the much more sweeping claim (which is unjustified) that the same can be said of all uses of 'good'. This is what he would have to show, if he wished to establish his contention that the common meaning of 'good' is descriptive. 'Good' often precedes words which are not functional. In such cases, in order to know what traits the thing in question would have to have in order to be called good, it is not sufficient to know the meaning of the word. We have also to know what standard is to be adopted for judging the goodness of this sort of thing; and this standard is not even partly (as in the case of functional words) revealed to us by the meaning of the word which follows 'good'. Thus, we may know, not only the meaning of 'good', but also the meaning of 'sunset' (and thus know the meaning of the whole expression, 'good sunset'), without thereby having determined for us the traits which a sunset must have in order to be called good.

[1] This example gives rise to much useful reflection; some materials for this reflection are to be found on p. 36 of *LM*, where a similar example occurs. For the connection between my use of the example and Geach's, see below, p. 35 n.

[2] *LM*, p. 100; cf. Geach, p. 38.

There is, indeed, general agreement among those who are interested in looking at sunsets, what a sunset has to be like to be called a good one (it has to be bright but not dazzling, and cover a wide area of sky with varied and intense colours, etc.); but this standard is not even hinted at in the meaning of 'sunset', let alone in that of 'good'.

It must be emphasised that this difference between the behaviour of 'good' when it precedes a functional word, and its behaviour when it precedes a non-functional word, is not due to any difference in the meaning of 'good' itself. We may say, roughly, that it means in both cases 'having the characteristic qualities (whatever they are) which are commendable in the kind of object in question'. The difference between the two cases is that the functional word does, and the non-functional word does not, give us clues as to what these qualities are. This is because, in classifying a thing as a hygrometer, for example, we have already determined that evaluation of it is to be according to a certain standard, whereas in classifying something else as a sunset we have not. Thus the word 'hygrometer' is, unlike the word 'sunset', not purely descriptive. To know the meaning of 'hygrometer', we do not only have to know what observable properties a thing must have to be called a hygrometer; we have also to know something about what would justify us in commending or condemning something as a hygrometer. None of this is true of 'sunset'; to know the meaning of 'sunset' we have merely to know that we can give this name to what we see in the western sky when the sun visibly sinks beneath the horizon.[1]

Now it is obviously Geach's intention that what he says about 'good' in general should be applicable to moral uses of the word. The question therefore arises whether the words which succeed 'good' in moral contexts are ever functional words. My own view is that the mere occurrence of a functional word after 'good' is normally an indication that the context is *not* a moral one. There are some possible exceptions to this rule; for instance, the phrase 'good example' occurs in moral contexts, and 'example' in such contexts is possibly a functional word,

---

[1] The explanation of the paradox that the expression 'good hygrometer' has a fixed *descriptive* meaning just because the two words composing it are both partly *evaluative* will be evident to anyone who compares *LM*, pp. 100–1, with ibid., pp. 36–7; the two evaluations 'cancel one another out'.

meaning 'thing to imitate'. I am not sure what account is to be given of this expression; but fortunately I do not, for the purposes of this argument, need to maintain that in moral contexts 'good' is never used with functional words, but only that it is sometimes used with non-functional words. For I shall then have shown that, at any rate in those contexts, neither 'good' itself, nor the whole expression in which it occurs, is purely descriptive. And thus I shall have shown that, if there is a common meaning of 'good' which it has in all cases, Geach's account of this common meaning is inadequate.

'He is a good man' is a moral judgement in some contexts, though in some it is not. If 'man' is being used (as it sometimes is) to mean 'soldier' or 'servant' (both functional words), the expression 'good man' is non-moral, just because the word 'man' is being used functionally. It is part of the definitions of a soldier and a servant that they have certain duties; a servant who acts contrary to his master's wishes or interests is *eo ipso* a bad servant, and a soldier whose conduct is conducive to the losing of wars by his side is *eo ipso* a bad soldier. But if 'man' is being used in the ordinary, general way to mean 'member of the human species', it is not functional; and this is the way in which it is used in moral contexts. I think that the same is true of the expression 'good human action' which Geach uses; but since this expression is not in common use, it is hard to be sure. At any rate, in the common expression 'good action', 'action' is not functional. One may know the meaning of 'action' without knowing anything which determines, even to the smallest degree, what actions are to be called good or bad. And if 'human', like 'man', is a non-functional word, the same will be true of 'human action'.

It is not, however, necessary for my argument to make any assumptions about what is or is not included in the meaning of the word 'man'. It will suffice to consider various things that *might* be included, and to notice the logical consequences of their inclusion. As often in philosophy, nothing here hangs upon the *actual* current use of words; but, *if* we decide to use them in a certain way, we must abide by the consequences. We might decide to mean by 'man' simply 'living creature having the following physical shape . . .' followed by a specification of his shape. If this were what we meant by 'man', the word would clearly not be functional, and so the whole expression 'good man' would not be descriptive. But I would be prepared to agree with Geach if he protested that we mean more by 'man' than this. For, as he has pointed out to me, there might be creatures having the same shape as man, but to whom, because they lacked certain intellectual capacities, for example the power of rational speech, we would not allow the name. True, we call by the name 'man' an offspring of human parents who lacks this power. But if we discovered a *race* of creatures who lacked this power, we might hesitate to call them men.

So far, Geach and I can perhaps agree. But it is one thing to say that by calling a creature a man we imply that he belongs to a species having certain *capacities*, and quite another thing to say that by so calling him we imply that he belongs to a species whose *specific good*[1] is of a certain kind. We might, for example, refuse to allow the name 'men' to a species of creatures who, though otherwise like the men we know, were psychologically incapable of lying, or murdering, or doing any other of the things commonly called sinful. We might say 'They aren't human; we would do better to call them "angels", or (if there are theological objections to that) by some new distinctive name'. If this were how we used the word 'man', the possession of these *powers* (of lying, murdering, etc.) would be part of the *ratio* of the word 'man', so used. But from this it would not follow that the exercise of these powers, or even their possession, is conducive to the specific good of man, or that to impair these powers or restrain their exercise (for example by a thorough-going moral education) is contrary to the specific good of man.[2]

If Geach wants to make it possible to draw from the meaning of 'man' conclusions about what is contrary to or conducive to a man's being a good man, he will have to include in the meaning of the word not only certain stipulations about the

---

[1] I take this expression from a letter of Geach's.

[2] Geach is the latest of a famous succession of thinkers who have systematically confused 'what a thing *can* (or, alternatively, *can typically*, or *does typically*) do', with the quite different notion 'what a thing *ought* to do (or, alternatively, what it is specifically *good* for it to do)'. Plato was of course the principal culprit. The word 'function' has perhaps been used to cover all these notions. The assimilation between them is only justified if we accept the assumed premiss *Natura (sive Deus) nihil facit inane*. Anyone who feels attracted by Geach's use of this kind of reasoning should first read Aristotle, *Politics* 1252 a 35, where a similar premiss is used in order to justify slavery and the subjection of women (cf. also 1253 a 9).

capacities of those entitled to the name 'man', but also something about what it is to be a *good* man. He will, in short, have to make 'man' into a functional word. Now let us suppose that Geach takes this liberty. Then the whole expression 'good man', and perhaps also such expressions as 'good human action', will receive fixed descriptive meanings. But he will have paid a severe penalty for this achievement. It will mean that what he says on p. 40 is no longer true: 'What a man cannot fail to be choosing is his manner of acting, so to call a manner of acting good or bad cannot but serve to guide action'. On the suggested definition of 'man', and hence of 'human', this will no longer be the case, if 'action' (as Geach implies in the first line of the paragraph from which this quotation comes) is short for 'human action'. For in choosing what to do I may be choosing, not within the class of comparison '*human* actions', but within some other, larger class. Similarly, if 'horse' is used as a functional word, meaning 'charger', a horse that throws his rider becomes *eo ipso* a bad one; but the *horse* might say to himself 'I'm not trying to be a horse in *that* sense; I'm only a solid-hoofed perissodactyl quadruped (*Equus caballus*), having a flowing mane and tail', and proceed to throw his rider without offence to anything except the rider's standards. For, though the meaning of the word 'charger' determines some of the qualities of a good charger, that of the word 'horse', in the more general definition given by the *O.E.D.*, does not; in this sense of 'horse', the question of what horses ought to do with themselves remains open. Just *because* the horse cannot choose but be a horse in this general sense, the fact that it is a horse in this general sense does not determine whether or not it ought to choose to be a good charger. It may not regard the choice before it as a choice, what sort of charger to be, but only, more generally, what sort of horse to be. The horsebreaker's art would be easy if one could turn horses into chargers by definition.

4   Ethics

1. *Introductory*

Out of the many sorts of inquiry for which the term 'ethics' has at one time or another been used, three groups of questions may be selected as the most important to distinguish from one another:

(1) *Moral questions:* for example, 'Ought I to do that?'; 'Is polygamy wrong?'; 'Is Jones a good man?' In this sense 'ethical' and 'moral' mean much the same. (2) *Questions of fact about people's moral opinions:* for example, 'What did Mohammed (or what does the British Middle Class, or what do I myself) in fact think (or say) about the rightness or wrongness of polygamy?' (3) *Questions about the meanings of moral words (for example, 'ought', 'right', 'good', 'duty'); or about the nature of the concepts or the 'things' to which these words 'refer':* for example, 'When Mohammed said that polygamy is not wrong, what was he saying?' These three sorts of questions being quite distinct, the use of the word 'ethics' to embrace attempts to answer all three is confusing, and is avoided by the more careful modern writers. No generally accepted terminology for making the necessary distinctions has yet emerged; but in this article we shall distinguish between (1) morals, (2) descriptive ethics and (3) ethics, corresponding to the three sorts of questions listed above. The case for confining the word 'ethics' (used without qualification) to the third sort of question is that ethics has usually been held to be a part of philosophy, and the third group of questions, which are analytical or logical inquiries, or, as older writers might say, metaphysical ones, is much more akin than the first two groups to other inquiries generally included in philosophy. Thus ethics (in the narrow sense) stands to morals in much the same relation as does the philosophy of science to science. The student of ethics will nevertheless have to get used to a variety of terminologies; he will find plain 'ethics' used for what we have just

Reprinted from *Encyclopedia of Western Philosophy and Philosophers,* ed. J. O. Urmson (Hutchinson, 1960).

called 'morals' ('normative ethics' is another term used for this); and he will find, for what we have just called 'ethics', the more guarded terms 'the logic of ethics', 'metaethics', 'theoretical ethics', 'philosophical ethics', and so on. Works called 'ethics' usually contain questions and answers of all three kinds, and the student of ethics must be prepared to find in them ambiguous remarks in which it is not clear *what* sort of question the writer is trying to answer. It is, for example, only too easy to confuse a moral statement with a descriptive ethical one, especially when one is talking about one's own moral views; but it is nevertheless vital to distinguish the moral judgement 'It would be wrong to do that' from the descriptive ethical statement 'I, as a matter of psychological fact, think that it would be wrong to do that'. The first task, therefore, for anybody who takes up the subject, is to learn to distinguish these three types of questions from one another; and for this purpose the following rules may be found helpful. A writer is making a *moral* statement if he is thereby *committing* himself to a moral view or standpoint; if not (that is, if he is merely writing in a detached way about moral views which are or may be held by himself or other people), it is either a *descriptive ethical* or an *ethical* statement; and this is normally indicated by the form of the statement, the moral words being 'insulated' by occurring inside a 'that'-clause or quotation-marks. Which of the two it is can be decided in the following way: if the truth of the statement depends on what moral opinions are *actually held* by people, it is a *descriptive ethical* statement; but if its truth depends only on what is *meant* by certain words, or on *what people would be saying if* they voiced certain moral opinions, it is an *ethical* statement. Thus, for example, ethics in the narrow sense is concerned directly neither with whether polygamy *is* wrong (a moral question) nor with whether anybody in fact thinks it is wrong (a descriptive ethical question) – though ethics may have a bearing on these two questions, as mathematics has on physics; it is concerned with the question, 'Precisely what is one saying if one says that polygamy is wrong' ?

2. *Relations between these Inquiries*

Throughout the history of the subject, the chief incentive to the undertaking of all three sorts of inquiry has been the hope of

establishing conclusions of the first kind (that is, moral conclusions) by means of a philosophical inquiry. It is from this
motive that inquiries of the second and especially the third
kinds have mostly been undertaken. Clearly the study of the
meaning of the moral words is closely related to the study of
what makes arguments containing them cogent or otherwise.
One of the best ways of obtaining a clear view of the subject is
to consider the mutual relations between these three kinds of
inquiry, and the bearing that they can have on one another.

(1) *Descriptive ethics and morals.* Some writers have proceeded
directly from descriptive ethical premisses to moral (normative
ethical) conclusions. For example, the Greek hedonist Eudoxus
argued that since everyone thought pleasure to be the good,
it must *be* the good. In a similar way some modern writers have
held that the task of the moral philosopher – the utmost he can
do by way of establishing moral conclusions – is to examine
carefully the opinions that are accepted by his society or by
himself and reduce them to some sort of system. This is to take
received opinions as data, and to regard as established a moral
system that can be shown to be consistent with them. This type
of argumentation will not, however, appear convincing to
anyone who considers the fact that a person (for example, in
the ancient world) might have said 'Everyone thinks that it is
legitimate to keep slaves, but may it not be wrong?' Universal
assent to a moral principle does not prove the principle; otherwise the moral reformer, who propounds for the first time a new
moral principle, could be put out of court all too easily. Still less
does it follow, from the fact that some limited set of people hold
some moral opinion, that that opinion is right.

(2) *Descriptive ethics and ethics proper.* The commonest way,
however, in which it has been sought to bring descriptive ethics
to bear on moral questions is not directly but indirectly. It has
been thought that a descriptive ethical inquiry might lead to
conclusions about the *meanings* of moral terms (conclusions, that
is to say, in ethics proper); and that in turn these might be used
to prove moral conclusions. Those who have argued in this way
have been attracted by a seductive analogy between moral
terms and other predicates and adjectives. For example, it
might be held possible to prove in the following way, to anyone
who disputed it, that post-boxes in England are red: we should
first establish by observation that everybody says that things are

red when they have a certain recognisable quality, and that they are not red when they do not have this quality; we should conclude from this that 'red' *means* 'having this quality'. This is the first step. We should then ask our disputant to observe that post-boxes in England have this same quality; and since we have already established that 'having this quality' is just what 'red' *means*, he can no longer deny that the post-boxes are red. It might be thought possible to use the same argument in ethics to prove, for example, that certain kinds of action are right. But unfortunately the analogy breaks down at both steps – at the step from descriptive ethics to ethics proper, and at the step from ethics to morals. That conclusions about what people *mean by* 'right', for example, cannot be proved by finding out what they *call* right, is evident from the case of the moral reformer just mentioned. If he said that slavery was not right, when slavery was one of the things universally agreed to be right, he would, if the proposed argument were valid, be like a man who said that post-boxes were not red when everybody agreed that they were red; we should be able to accuse such a man of misusing the word 'red' – for 'red' *means* the colour which post-boxes are, so how can he deny that they are red ? But the moral reformer can deny that slavery is right while still using the word 'right' in the same sense as that in which his contemporaries, who think that slavery is right, are using it. This example shows that there is an important difference between moral words and words like 'red' – a difference which invalidates the superficially plausible argument from descriptive-ethical premisses to conclusions about the meanings of moral words.

(3) *Ethics and morals.* But the second step in the proposed argument is also invalid, for a very similar reason. We cannot, even if we can establish the meaning of the moral words, pass from this to conclusions of substance about moral questions. This may be shown by the following example: suppose that there are two people who know everything about a certain action (including its circumstances and consequences), and still dispute, as they may, about whether it was wrong. Since they are in dispute, they must be using the word 'wrong' with the same meaning; for if this were not so, there would be no real dispute, only a verbal confusion. But since they can continue to dispute, even though they are in agreement about the meaning of the word, it follows that knowledge of the meaning

of the word cannot by itself, or even in conjunction with what
they both know about the action, determine whether the action
is wrong. Some *other* difference must remain between them (a
moral difference) which is neither a difference about what the
action is (for this they know in the fullest detail) nor about
the meaning of 'wrong' (for about this they are agreed). The
plausible argument which we have just rejected is a particular
application of a type of argument often used in philosophy, and
known as 'the argument from the paradigm case'. Without
discussing here whether the argument is cogent in other fields,
we can see that it is not in ethics. The assumption that this
argument has unrestricted force is linked with the assumption
that to discover the use of a word is always to discover to what
things it is correctly applied. This is not true of words like 'is'
and 'not'; and it seems not to be true of moral words either. This
assumption (to take another example) leaves us with no way of
distinguishing between the uses of the two sets of words 'Shut
the door' and 'You are going to shut the door'; for all the words
in both sets, in so far as they 'apply' to anything, apply to the
same things.

3. *Naturalism*

The arguments so far considered and rejected all exhibit a
common feature. In them, moral conclusions are allegedly
derived from premises which are not themselves moral judgements: in the one case the premiss was a statement of sociological
fact about what people think on a moral question; in the other
it was a statement of linguistic fact about how (with what
meaning) people use a certain word, together with another
premiss giving the description of an action whose wrongness is in
dispute. This feature is common to a great many arguments
which have been used by ethical thinkers; and it has been
frequently stated that any argument which derives moral conclusions from non-moral premises must be invalid. A famous
statement to this effect was made by Hume in *Treatise of Human
Nature* (1739–40) III I i. Hume based his rejection of such
arguments on the general logical principle that a valid argument cannot proceed from premises to some 'new affirmation'
not contained, at any rate implicitly, in the premises. The
correctness of Hume's view ('no *ought* from an *is*') depends,

therefore, on the assumption that moral judgements contain an element in their meaning (the essentially moral element) which is not equivalent, even implicitly, to anything in the conjunction of the premises. It is this assumption which is challenged by those ethical theories known as naturalist. The term 'naturalist' has been used in a variety of ways, but will be used here as follows: an ethical theory is naturalistic if, and only if, it holds that moral judgements are equivalent in meaning to statements of non-moral fact.

It must be noted that, on this definition, a statement of moral opinion (that is to say a statement in the first of the three classes listed at the beginning of this article) cannot be called naturalistic; for naturalism is a view about the meanings of moral terms, and nobody is committed to any form of it who confines himself to merely *using* moral terms without taking up a view about their meaning, definition or analysis. In general, no view can be naturalistic unless, in the statement of the view, the moral words occur inside quotation marks or a 'that'-clause or are *mentioned* (not used) in some other way, and remarks are made about their meaning or their equivalence to other expressions. That is to say, only statements in ethics proper, as contrasted with descriptive ethics and with morals, can be naturalistic. Thus the view that the right action (the action which ought to be done) in a given situation is that which would produce the greatest balance of pleasure over pain, is not naturalistic, since it does not seek to *define* 'right', but only to say what actions *are* right. To be a naturalist, a utilitarian of this sort would have to hold, in addition, that his view was true in virtue of the meaning of 'right' – that is to say, that 'right' *meant* 'producing the greatest balance of pleasure over pain'. If he refrains from trying to prove his theory in this way, 'refutations of naturalism' pass over his head.

It must also be noticed that, on this definition of naturalism, to call a definition of a moral word 'naturalistic' does not imply that the properties in terms of which it is being defined are empirical, that is, perceived by the five senses. As Moore, who coined the expression 'the naturalistic fallacy', observed, the same 'fallacy', as he thought it was, is committed if the properties are 'properties of supersensible reality', given only that they are not moral properties. Thus a philosopher who *defines* 'right' as meaning 'in accordance with the will of God' is, in this sense, a naturalist, unless the word 'God' itself is held to be implicitly a moral term. The most important argument by which Moore sought to 'refute naturalism' may be restated as follows, using the example just quoted: if 'right' meant the same as 'in accordance with the will of God', then, 'whatever is in accordance with the will of God is right' would mean the same as 'whatever is in accordance with the will of God is in accordance with the will of God'; but according to our actual use of the words it seems to mean more than this mere tautology. (Note that, as before, there is nothing in this argument which forces anybody to abandon the *moral* view that whatever is in accordance with the will of God and only what is in accordance with it is right. It is only the attempt to make this view true by definition which is naturalistic.) It has been held, though not by Moore, that what is wrong with naturalistic definitions is that they leave out the commendatory or prescriptive element in the meaning of words such as 'right' and 'good' (see below).

4. *Intuitionism*

The work of Moore convinced most philosophers that naturalistic definitions of moral terms had to be ruled out. But Moore and his immediate followers showed a great reluctance to abandon what had been the traditional view of the way in which words have meaning. It was taken for granted that the way to explain the meaning of an adjective, for example, was to identify the property which it 'stands for' or 'is the name of'; all adjectives have the same logical function, that of 'standing for' a property, and the differences between them are not differences in logical character, but simply differences between the properties for which they 'stand'. When, therefore, it became accepted that moral adjectives did not stand for 'natural' (that is, non-moral) properties, it was concluded that they must stand for peculiar moral properties, thought to be discerned by 'intuition'.

There are two main forms of ethical intuitionism. According to the first, we are supposed to intuite the rightness, goodness, etc., of concrete individual acts, people, etc.; general moral principles are arrived at by a process of induction, that is, by generalisation from a large number of these instances. According to the second, what we intuite are the general principles themselves (for example, 'promise-breaking is wrong'); by applying these, we ascertain the moral properties of individual acts and people. The second view has the merit of emphasising a very important fact about the logical character of moral words, namely that the moral adjectives, etc., differ from most other adjectives in the following way: we call a thing 'red', for example, because of its redness and nothing else; it could be similar in every other way and yet not be red. But when we call a person 'good' or an act 'right', we call them good or right *because* they have certain other characteristics – for example, an act is called wrong because it is an act of promise-breaking, or good because it is the act of helping a blind man across a road. The intuitionists sometimes express this feature of moral adjectives by saying that they are the 'names' of 'consequential' or 'supervenient' properties. Even if we reject the idea that all adjectives have meaning by being the names of properties, this remains an important discovery. It has sometimes been thought that Hume's 'no *ought* from an *is*' was a denial that we can, for example, call an act good *because* it is an act of a certain kind. This is a misunderstanding; what Hume was denying was that it *logically followed*, from an act's being of a certain kind, that it is good. The difference is crucial, but obscure. It has been one of the main problems of recent ethics to give a satisfactory account of the connexion between, for example, goodness and what were called 'good-making characteristics'. The intuitionists reject the naturalist explanation of this connexion as due to an equivalence in meaning between moral words and words describing the characteristics of things in virtue of which we apply moral words to them. But they give no adequate positive account of the connexion, contenting themselves, for the most part, with saying that it is a 'synthetic necessary' connexion discerned by 'intuition'. The explanatory force of this account is impaired by the failure to say clearly what 'intuition' is or what is meant by 'synthetic necessary connexion'.

But the chief argument brought against ethical intuitionism of all sorts is the following, which is to be compared with that in section 2 (3). Intuition is supposed to be a way of knowing, or determining definitively and objectively, the truth or falsity of a given moral judgement. But suppose that two people differ on a moral question, and that both, as may well happen, claim to intuite the correctness of their own views. There is then no way left of settling the question, since each can accuse the other of being defective in intuition, and there is nothing about the intuitions themselves to settle which it is. It is often objected further, that what 'moral intuitions' people have will depend on their various moral upbringings and other contingent causes. In fact, the intuitionists, who often claim to be 'objectivists', belie this claim by appealing to a faculty of intuition which is unavoidably subjective. This illustrates the extreme difficulty, to be referred to below, of stating any clear distinction between 'objective' and 'subjective' in this field. Intuitionism enjoyed a wide popularity in the early years of this century; but it has now been abandoned even by some of its prominent supporters. Writers on ethics have tended, either to revert to some form of naturalism, open or disguised, or to pass on to one of the kinds of view, to be described below, which recognise that 'good', 'right', etc., have, logically, a quite different role from that of other adjectives, and that it may be misleading to call them 'the names of properties'.

5. *Relativism and Subjectivism*

Great confusion has been caused in ethics by lumping together, under the title 'subjectivism', theories which are quite different from one another. Before considering subjectivism proper, we must first distinguish from it the *moral* view which is best called *relativism*. A typical relativist holds that we ought to do that, and that only, which we *think* we ought to do; on this theory, the mere having of a certain moral opinion by a man or a society makes that moral opinion correct for that man or society. Since this is a *moral* doctrine and not an *ethical* one (that is, since it says what we ought to do, not what 'ought' means) it is not naturalistic (see above); but it is open to the objection that it makes it impossible to say that another man's moral judgement is wrong – indeed, it has the paradoxical consequence that two people who differ about a moral question must both be right. This seems to be at variance with the common use of the moral words; we have here an illustration of a way in which ethics (the study of the uses of the moral words) can have a negative bearing on a moral question – it enables us to *rule out* a moral view as involving logical paradox, but not to *prove* one. It may also be objected to relativism that it does not do what a moral principle is expected to do, viz. guide us in making our decisions on particular moral questions. For if I am wondering what to do, it is no use being told that I ought to do what I think I ought to do; for the trouble is that I do not know what to think. Relativism is mentioned, not for its own value, but because confusion of other views with it has bedevilled nearly all discussion of the views which we are about to consider. These are by contrast all ethical views (that is, views about the meanings of the moral words). They do not commit the holder of them to the acceptance or rejection of any substantive moral opinions.

The first is a form of naturalism, which is not now often avowedly held, but dates from a time when it was thought that a moral sentence must have meaning in the same way as other indicative sentences, viz. by being used to state that a certain object possesses a certain property (see above, section 4). It being unplausible, for many reasons (some of which have been given in section 3), to hold that the properties in question are 'objective' properties of objects, it was suggested that they are 'subjective' properties – that is, properties of being related in certain ways to states of mind of the maker of the statement in question. Thus 'He is a good man' was held to mean 'He, as a matter of psychological fact, arouses in me a certain mental state (for example, a feeling of approval)'. This theory makes a moral judgement equivalent to a descriptive ethical statement (see above, section 1). If it is taken literally, it is open to the objection that it makes moral disagreement impossible. For if two people say, one that a man is a good man, and the other that he is not, they are, on this view, not disagreeing with each other; for one of them means that he (the speaker) is in a certain mental state, and the other means that *he* (the second speaker) is not in that state; and between these statements there is no contradiction.

Because of this objection, the view has been generally abandoned in favour of others which hold that in a moral judgement we are not giving information about our mental state, but engaging in a use of language different from the giving of information. This development has been part of the recent realisation by philosophers that it is a mistake to regard all kinds of sentences as having the same logical character and role. For at least two reasons it is best to confine the name 'subjectivism' to the view just considered, and not to extend it to those described below. First of all, the terms 'objective' and 'subjective' have a tolerably clear meaning, and draw a graspable distinction, when they are used to mark the difference between statements of 'objective' fact about objects, and statements of 'subjective' fact about the speaker (though even here there might be confusion; for in a sense it is an objective fact that the mind of the speaker is in a certain state). But the distinction gets lost when moral judgements are held not to be statements of fact, in the narrow sense, at all. This may be seen by comparing the case of imperatives (though it is not suggested that moral judgements resemble these in all respects). An imperative expresses neither an objective statement nor a subjective statement, since it does not express a statement at all, nor does it express a 'subjective command'; for it is hard to understand what this would be. So, if it be asked 'Is the command "Shut the door" *about* the door or *about* the mind of the speaker ?', the answer, in so far as the question is meaningful, must be 'About the door'. And in the same way the moral judgement 'He is a good man' may be held to be, in the strongest possible sense, 'about' the man in question, and not about the mind of the speaker, even by someone who holds that it is not (in the narrow sense) a *statement of fact* about the man. Thus criticisms of the theories to be described in the next section, on the ground that they turn moral judgements into remarks about the mind of the speaker, are misdirected, and should be reserved for subjectivism as described in the present section. The same applies to the criticism that these theories 'make what is right depend on what the speaker thinks is right'.

Secondly, the division between those views which hold that moral judgements are used to give some sort of information, and those which hold that they have a quite different function, is the most fundamental in ethics, and should not be concealed by using a term which straddles it. Views of the first sort (for example, all the ethical views so far considered) are called 'descriptivist'; views of other kinds, including those considered in the rest of this article, are called 'non-descriptivist'.

6. *Emotivism*

Though emotivism was, historically, the first kind of non-descriptivism to be canvassed, it is a mistake to think of it as the only kind, or even as commanding general support among non-descriptivists at the present time. It is common even now for non-descriptivists of all kinds to be misleadingly called 'emotivists', even though their theories do not depend on any reference to the emotions. Emotivism proper embraces a variety of views, which may be held concurrently. According to the best-known, moral judgements have it as their function to 'express' or 'evince' the moral emotions (for example, approval) of the speaker. According to another version, their use is to arouse or evoke similar emotions in the person to whom they are addressed, and so stimulate him to actions of the kind approved. A. J. Ayer when he wrote *Language, Truth and Logic* (1936), which contains the most famous exposition of emotivism, attributed both these functions to moral judgements; but he has since abandoned emotivism, though remaining a non-descriptivist. C. L. Stevenson put forward a kindred view, with the difference that, instead of the word 'emotion', he most commonly used the word 'attitude'. An attitude was usually thought of by him as a disposition to be in certain mental states or to do certain kinds of actions. Stevenson's 'attitudes' are much closer to the 'moral principles' of the older philosophers (especially Aristotle) than is usually noticed by those who use the misleading 'objectivist-subjectivist' classification. Stevenson made the important qualification to his view that, besides their 'emotive meaning', moral judgements may also have a 'descriptive meaning'. In one of his several 'patterns of analysis' the meaning of a moral judgement is analysed into two components: (1) a non-moral assertion about, for example, an act (explicable naturalistically in terms of empirical properties of the act); and (2) a specifically moral component (the emotive meaning) whose presence prevents a naturalistic account being given of the meaning of the whole judgement. This specifically moral element in the meaning is the function which these judgements have of *expressing* attitudes and *persuading* or *influencing* people to adopt them, towards the act described. Stevenson's views did not, of course, find favour with descriptivists; and even non-descriptivists who have written after him, while recognising the seminal importance of his work, have for the most part rejected the implied irrationalism of the view that the only specifically moral element in the meaning of moral terms is their emotive force. This, it has been felt, makes moral judgements too like rhetoric or propaganda, and does insufficient justice to the possibility of reasoned argument about moral questions. If moral argument is possible, there must be *some* logical relations between a moral judgement and other moral judgements, even if Hume was right to hold that a moral judgement is not derivable from statements of non-moral fact. Stevenson has some important things to say about moral arguments, but his account of them has been generally held to be inadequate.

7. *Outstanding Problems*

Most of the main problems which occupy ethical thinkers at the present time arise from the complexity of the meaning of moral terms, which combines two very different elements.

(1) *The evaluative or prescriptive meaning* (these more non-committal terms are now often preferred to Stevenson's 'emotive meaning'). It is not necessary, and probably false, to attribute to moral judgements, as such, any impulsive or causative force or power to *make* or *induce us to* do what they enjoin; but even descriptivists sometimes admit that moral judgements have the function of *guiding* conduct. It is indeed fairly evident that in many typical cases we ask, for example, 'What ought I to do?' because we have to decide what to do, and think that the answer to the 'ought' question has a bearing on our decision greater and more intimate than that possessed by answers to questions of non-moral fact. To take another example, it is fairly evident that there is an intimate connexion between thinking A better than B, and preferring A to B, and between the latter and being disposed to choose A rather than B. This intimate connexion is emphasised in the old tag (whose substance goes back to Socrates): 'Whatever is sought, is sought under the appearance of its being good'. It would follow from this that to call a thing good is thereby to offer guidance about choices; and the same might be said of the other moral terms. Descriptivists, however, refuse to admit that this feature is part of the *meaning* of moral terms.

Their principal opponents, who may be called 'prescriptivists', hold that it *is* part of the meaning. Moral judgements, on this view, share with imperatives the characteristic that to utter one is to commit oneself, directly or indirectly, to some sort of precept or prescription about actual or conceivable decisions or choices. In typical cases, disagreement with a moral judgement is displayed by failure to act on it – as when some-one has told me that the right thing to do is such and such, and I immediately do the opposite. Such a view does not, like the emotive theory, make moral argument impossible; for accor-ding to some prescriptivists logical relations may hold between prescriptions as well as between ordinary statements.

Prescriptivists have to face, like Socrates, the difficulty that in cases of so-called 'weakness of will' we may choose to do something which we think bad or wrong. The most promising line for prescriptivists to take in answer to this objection is to point out that in such cases either the chooser is *unable* to resist the temptation (as is indicated by the expression '*weakness* of will'; cf. also St Paul, Romans 7: 23); or else he thinks the thing bad or wrong only in some weaker, conventional sense, having the descriptive meaning of 'bad' or 'wrong' but lacking their prescriptive force.

(2) *The descriptive meaning.* The second main feature of moral judgements is that which distinguishes them from imperatives: whenever we make a moral judgement about, for example, an act, we must make it because of *something about* the act, and it always makes sense to ask what this something is (though it may be hard to put a reply into words). This (although it has been denied by some recent thinkers) follows from the 'consequential' character of moral 'properties' (see above, section 4). To every particular moral judgement, then, there corresponds a universal judgement to the effect that a certain feature of the thing judged is, so far as it goes, a reason for making a certain moral judgement about it. For instance, if I say that a particular act is good because it is the act of helping a blind man across a road, I seem to be adhering thereby to the universal judgement that it is good to help blind people across roads (and not merely this particular blind man across this particular road). Those who accept this argument may be called 'universalists'; and their opponents, who do not, may be called 'particularists'. A universalist is not committed to the view that, if it is a good act to help a blind man across a road on this occasion, it would be a good act on all occasions (for example, it would not be a good act if the blind man was known to be hopelessly lost and his destination lay on this side of the

road); he is committed only to the view that it would be a good act in the absence of something to make a difference between the two acts – something more than the mere numerical difference between the acts.

The universalist thesis is closely connected with the thesis that moral judgements, besides their function as prescriptions, have also a descriptive meaning (see above, section 6). On this view, in calling an act, for example, good, we are commending it (the prescriptive element in the meaning), but commending it because of something about it. These two elements are well summarised by the *Oxford English Dictionary*'s first definition of 'good': 'The most general adjective of commendation, implying the existence in a high, or at least satisfactory, degree of characteristic qualities which are either admirable in themselves or useful for some purpose'. The word 'characteristic' is important; it draws attention to the fact that the word which follows 'good' makes a difference to the qualities which a thing has to have in order to be called good (for example, a good strawberry does not have to have the same qualities as a good man). In the case of some words (for example, 'knife'), if we know what they mean, we know some of the conditions that have to be fulfilled before we can call a thing of that kind good. Some philosophers (for example Plato and Aristotle) have held that the same is true of all words – that, for example, if we could determine 'the nature of man' we should therefore be able to say what makes a man a good man. But this type of argument may be based on a false analogy between words like 'man' and words like 'knife'.

A more promising way of bringing the universalist thesis to bear on moral arguments (and thus to some extent satisfying those who insist that ethical studies should be relevant to moral questions) is that exemplified by the 'Golden Rule' and worked out in some detail (though obscurely) by Kant and his followers. In certain cases it may be a powerful argument, if a man is contemplating some act, to ask what it is about the act which makes him call it right, and whether, if some other act possessed the same features, but his own role in it were different, he would judge it in the same way. This type of argument occurs in two famous passages of Scripture (2 Samuel 12:7 and Matthew 18:32). It has been held that a judgement is not a *moral* judgement unless the speaker is prepared to 'universalise his maxim'. But this raises the vexed question of the criteria for calling judgements 'moral judgements' – a question which is beyond the scope of this article.

This question, and the whole problem of the relation between the prescriptive and the descriptive elements in the meaning of moral judgements, continues to tax ethical thinkers. It has been impossible in this article to do more than sketch the principal issues and give some account of their origin.

5   Descriptivism

I

The term 'Descriptivism' was first suggested to me by a phrase of the late Professor Austin's. He refers in two places to what he calls the 'descriptive fallacy' of supposing that some utterance is descriptive when it is not;[1] and, although I agree with him that the word might mislead, it will serve. 'Descriptivism', then, can perhaps be used as a generic name for philosophical theories which fall into this fallacy. I shall, however, be discussing, not descriptivism in general, but the particular variety of it which is at present fashionable in ethics; and I shall not attempt to discuss all forms even of ethical descriptivism, nor, even, all the arguments of those descriptivists whom I shall consider. A sample will be all that there is time for. I cannot claim that my own arguments are original – I am in particularly heavy debt to Mr Urmson and Professor Nowell-Smith; but if old mistakes are resuscitated, it is often impossible to do more than restate, in as clear a way as possible, the old arguments against them. Philosophical mistakes are like dandelions in the garden; however carefully one eradicates them there are sure to be some more next year, and it is difficult to think of novel ways of getting rid of their familiar faces. '*Naturalitas expellas furca, tamen usque recurrent.*' But in fact the best implement is still the old fork invented by Hume.

An essential condition for the use of this tool is that there should be a distinction between description and evaluation; and, since the more sophisticated of modern descriptivists sometimes seek to impugn this distinction, I must start by establishing its existence, though I shall not have time to add to what I have said elsewhere about its nature.[2] This problem is

Reprinted from *Proceedings of the British Academy*, XLIX (1963).

[1] *Philosophical Papers*, p. 71; cf. *How to do things with words*, p. 3.

[2] *The Language of Morals (LM)*, esp. chap. 7; *Freedom and Reason (FR)*, pp. 22–7, 51, 56.

very like that concerning the distinction between analytic and synthetic (indeed, it is an offshoot of that problem). Both distinctions are useful – indeed essential – tools of the philosopher, and it is no bar to their use that we have not yet achieved a completely clear formal elucidation of their nature.

The fundamental distinction is not that between descriptive and evaluative *terms*, but that between the descriptive and evaluative meaning which a single term may have in a certain context. In order to establish that there is a distinction between descriptive and evaluative meaning, it is not necessary to deny the existence of cases in which it is difficult to say whether a term is being used evaluatively or not. There is a clear distinction between a heap of corn and no corn at all, even though it is hard to say just when the corn that I am piling up has become a heap.[1] The descriptive and evaluative meaning of a term in a given context may be tied to it with varying degrees of tightness (we may be more, or less, sure that one or other of them would or would not get detached if we were faced with varying instances of its use: for example, if the cause to which a man was contributing large sums of money were one which I considered not good but pernicious, would I still say that he was generous ?). But for all that, the distinction between descriptive and evaluative meaning may be a perfectly sustainable one.

II

We can show that such a distinction exists, at any rate, if we can isolate one of these two sorts of meaning in a given context, and show that it does not exhaust the meaning of the term in that context. Suppose, for example, that we can show that in a certain context a term has descriptive meaning; and suppose that we can isolate this descriptive meaning by producing another term which could be used in the same context with the same descriptive meaning, but such that the two terms differ in that one has evaluative meaning and the other not; then we shall have established that there can be these two different components in a term's meaning.

Let us suppose that somebody says that a certain wine (let us

[1] See Cicero, *Lucullus*, 16; Sextus Empiricus, *Adv. Math.* i 69, 80 and *Hyp. Pyrrh.* ii 253.

call it 'Colombey-les-deux-églises 1972') is a good wine. I think it will be obvious that he says that it is a good wine *because* it has a certain taste, bouquet, body, strength, etc. (I shall say 'taste' for short). But it is equally clear that we do not have a name for precisely the taste which this wine has. A descriptivist might therefore argue as follows (thereby committing the fashionable fallacy of *nullum nomen nullum nominandum*): there is nothing more we can say about this wine, by way of telling somebody what is good about it, or what makes us call it good (which would be to give the descriptive meaning of 'good' in this context); we can only repeat that it is good. It is good because it tastes as it does, admittedly; but this is like saying that a thing is red because it looks as it does. How else could we describe the way it tastes than by saying that it is good? Therefore the description cannot be detached from the evaluation, and the distinction is rendered ineffective.

In this instance, such an argument would not carry conviction. If a descriptivist tried to show, by this means, that the descriptive meaning of 'good' in this context could not be isolated, we should no doubt answer that the difficulty lies only in the non-existence of a *word* for the quality that we are seeking to isolate. But this does not matter, provided that it is possible to coin a word and give it a meaning. This I shall now show how to do. I may point out in passing that, if we did not have the words 'sweet', 'juicy', 'red', 'large', and a few more, it would be impossible, without inventing words, to isolate the descriptive meaning of 'good' in the phrase 'good strawberry'; but this would not stop us saying that the phrase has as a descriptive meaning distinct from its evaluative meaning. We should just have to coin a word meaning 'like this strawberry in respect of taste, texture, size, etc.'; and this is what I am now going to do in the 'wine' case.

Let us invent a word, 'ϕ', to stand for that quality of the wine which makes us call it a good wine. The quality is, as I have explained, a complex one. Will you allow me to suppose, also, that (as is not improbable) by the time 1972 wines of this sort begin to be good, the science of aromatics (if that is the right name) will have advanced enough to put the wine-snobs out of business; that is to say, that it will have become possible to manufacture by chemical means additives which, put into cheap wines, will give to them tastes indistinguishable by any human palate from those of expensive wines. We should then have a chemical recipe for producing liquid tasting ϕ. This would make it easy (though even without such a scientific advance it would be perfectly possible) to teach somebody to recognise the ϕ taste by lining up samples of liquids tasting ϕ, and others having different tastes, and getting him to taste them, telling him in each case whether the sample tasted ϕ or not. It is worth noticing that I could do this whether or not he was himself disposed to think that these liquids tasted good, or that, if they were wines, they were good wines. He could, that is to say, learn the meaning of 'ϕ' quite independently of his own estimation of the merit of wines having that taste.

It is possible, indeed, that, if he did think that wines having that taste were good wines, he might mistake my meaning; he might think that 'ϕ wine' (the expression whose meaning I was trying to explain to him) meant the same as 'good wine'. It is always possible to make mistakes when a person is trying to explain to one the meaning of a word. But the mistake could be guarded against. I might say to him, 'I want you to understand that, in calling a wine ϕ, I am not thereby commending it or praising it in any way, any more than it is commending it or praising it to say that it is produced by this chemical recipe; I am indeed (for such is my preference) disposed to commend wines which have this taste; but in simply saying that a wine is ϕ I am not thereby commending it any more than I should be if I said that it tasted like vinegar or like water. If my preference (and for that matter everybody else's) changed in such a way that a wine tasting like this was no longer thought any good, and we could do nothing with it but pour it down the drain, we could still go on describing it as ϕ.'

Now it seems to me that the descriptivist argument which we are considering depends on what I have just said being quite unintelligible. If a man can understand the explanation of the meaning of 'ϕ', he must reject the descriptivist argument. For if the explanation works, then it is possible to explain the meaning of 'ϕ' ostensively as a descriptive expression; and when this has been done, we can separate out the descriptive from the evaluative meaning of the expression 'good wine' in the sentence 'Colombey 1972 is a good wine'. For it will be possible for two people to agree that Colombey 1972 tastes ϕ, but disagree about whether it is a good wine; and this shows (which is all that I am trying to show) that there is more to the statement that Colombey 1972 is a good wine than to the statement that Colombey 1972 is a wine which tastes ϕ. The more is, of course, the commendation; but I shall not in this lecture try to explain what this is, since I have done my best elsewhere.

This answer to the descriptivist argument is not, as might be thought at first hearing, circular. It is true that I introduced into it the distinction between commendation and description, which was what I was trying to establish; but I did not merely assume it as a premiss in my argument – I produced a clear example in which we could not do without it. What I did was to ask, 'Was it possible to understand what I was saying when I explained to the man that to call a thing ϕ is not thereby to commend or praise it, any more than it is praise or commendation to say that it tastes like the product of a certain chemical recipe, or that it tastes like vinegar or water?' And the premiss which I put into the argument was that this was perfectly intelligible. A determined descriptivist might at this point protest 'It isn't intelligible to me'; but I can only ask you whether, if he said this, he would not be professing to find unintelligible a distinction which we all know perfectly well how to operate (a familiar habit of philosophers). The distinction has, indeed, to be elucidated, and this is the task of moral philosophy; but it exists.

III

This 'wine' case is one where the difficulty arises because there is no word available having the descriptive meaning of 'good' in a certain context without its evaluative meaning. But a very similar difficulty arises when, as in most moral and aesthetic cases, there is no *one* word which has just the descriptive meaning that we want, but a multitude of possible ways of describing, in greater or less detail, the sort of thing that we have in mind. Here what is required is not ostensive definition (though that may help) but a long story. It is, for example, very hard to say what it is about a particular picture which makes us call it a good one; but nevertheless what makes us call it a good one is a series of describable characteristics combined in just this way. We can see this quite clearly if we think of the painter himself building up the picture – putting in features and then perhaps painting them out again and trying something else. There is no doubt whatever that what makes him satisfied or dissatisfied is something there on the canvas which is certainly describable in neutral terms (e.g. he has a lot of things round the edge of the picture which draw the eye, but no feature in the middle which does so). Or, to take a simpler example, let us suppose that the painter is somebody like Kandinsky, and that the only thing that dissatisfies him about the picture is the precise colour of one of the exactly-drawn circular patches near the top right-hand corner. Suppose then that the painter is suddenly and incurably paralysed, but wants to finish the picture; can he not get a pupil to alter the colour for him, telling him, in neutral descriptive terms, just what paints to mix in what proportions and where to put the resulting mixture in order to make it a better picture ? The paralysed painter would not have to say 'Make the picture better' or 'Make the circular patch in the top right-hand corner a better colour'; he could tell the pupil just how to do these things.

If, instead of asking what makes a man call *this* picture a good one, we ask what in general makes him call pictures (or wines or men) good ones, the position becomes even more complicated. But in principle it remains true that the descriptive meaning which the man attaches to the expression 'good picture' could be elicited, as a very complex conjunction and disjunction of characteristics, by questioning him sufficiently closely about a sufficiently large number of pictures.[1] For to have a settled taste in pictures is to be disposed to think pictures good which have certain characteristics. That such a process would reveal a good deal about his taste to the man himself does not affect the argument; the process of rendering articulate the grounds of evaluation is always a revealing one. If his evaluations have been made on vague or uncertain grounds, as will be the case with a man whose taste is not well developed, the process of trying to explain the grounds may well cause the evaluations themselves to change in the course of being made articulate. This again is irrelevant to the argument; for nobody wants to maintain that

[1] Though not competent to judge of such matters, I do not find the experiments described by Prof. H. J. Eysenck, *Sense and Nonsense in Psychology*, chap. 8, at all incredible, though I do not agree with his interpretation of them.

the descriptive meaning attached to people's evaluations is in all cases precise or cut-and-dried.

Lest you should think that I have been talking about pictures simply in order to make a logical point about value-judgements, I should like to say that there seems to me to be a lesson, in all this, about how to improve one's appreciation of works of art. In so far as I have attained to any articulate appreciation of any sorts of works of art – or of anything else which has aesthetic merit – it has been by trying to formulate to myself what I find good or bad about particular works, or about the works of a particular style or period. This is, of course, no substitute for the completely inarticulate absorption in a work – say a piece of music – which alone makes art worth while; but analysis does undoubtedly help. I have derived much more profit from looking at pictures and buildings, listening to music, etc., and asking myself what it is about them that I find worth while, than I have from reading the works of critics; and when critics have helped me, it has been by doing the same sort of thing, i.e. drawing attention to and characterising particular features of works of art which contribute to their excellence. I think that many descriptivists would agree with me about this. But unless what I have said is true (viz. that the descriptive meaning of 'good' in a given context can always in principle be given) critics would be unable to tell us why they think certain works of art good; they would just have to go on repeating that they are good.

IV

Morality is in these respects quite like aesthetics. There are certain ways of behaving, describable in perfectly neutral terms, which make us commend people as, for example, courageous. Citations for medals do not simply say that the recipient behaved courageously; they give descriptive details; and though these, for reasons of brevity, often themselves contain evaluative terms, this need not be the case, and in a good citation it is the neutral descriptions which impress. They impress us because we already have the standards of values according to which to do *that* sort of thing is to display outstanding merit.

A descriptivist might object to this argument that in some of my examples, although it is perfectly easy to say what the *descriptive* meaning of the term in question is, there is no separately discernible *evaluative* meaning. For example, it might be claimed that if we have said that the man has done what he has done, then we have said, implicitly, that he has been courageous; and if 'courageous' is a term of commendation, we have commended him. The commendation is simply the description. This I think to be false. With the standards of values that we have, and which it is natural for us to have in our historical circumstances (or perhaps in any likely historical circumstances), we shall all be disposed to commend such a man. But the commendation is a further step which we are not logically compelled to take. A man who said that such behaviour did not make a man any better would be morally eccentric, but not logically at fault. I have argued this point elsewhere.[1]

It follows that it is possible for two people without logical absurdity to agree about the description but disagree about the evaluation – though it would not affect my argument if nobody ever actually disagreed. And therefore the distinction between evaluative and descriptive meanings is not impugned.

V

I have sought to establish that there is this distinction, because I shall need it later. I shall now go on to deal with some particular descriptivist arguments. Most of the arguments which I shall be discussing have a feature in common: namely that the descriptivism which they seek to establish is of a very minimal kind. That is to say, they seek to establish only that there are *some* logical restrictions upon what we can call good, right, etc. They fall far short of attempting to prove anything that could be helpful to us when faced with any serious moral problem, as will be at once apparent to anyone who tries to use the types of reasoning proposed in any actual moral perplexity. But in this lecture I shall address myself mainly to arguments for these very weak forms of descriptivism, because they might seem more difficult to refute.

Consider the following argument. It is not possible, it might

[1] *FR*, pp. 187–9.

be said, to think *anything* good, or good of its kind, just as it is not possible to want *anything*; it is possible to want or to think good only such things as are thought to be either the subjects of what have been called 'desirability characterisations', or else means to attaining them. This expression 'desirability characterisations' comes from Miss Anscombe's book *Intention*, pp. 66 ff.; but I hesitate to ascribe the argument itself to her, because, as I shall show, the expression admits of at least two quite different interpretations, and I am not sure in which sense, if either, she was using the term; and therefore I am not sure which of two possible versions of the argument, if either, she would support. Since, however, although both versions are perfectly valid, neither proves anything from which I wish to dissent, I shall not try to do more than clear up the ambiguity – an ambiguity which has, I think, led some people to suppose that the argument does prove something with which a prescriptivist like myself would have to disagree.

The first way of taking the expression 'desirability characterisation' is to take it as meaning 'a description of that about the object which makes it an object of desire'. If I may be allowed to revert to my previous example: suppose that I want some Colombey 1972, or think it a good wine, because it tastes ϕ; then to say that it tastes ϕ is to give the required desirability characterisation. If this is how the phrase is to be taken, then the argument shows that whenever we think something good, we do so because of something about it. Since I have often maintained the same position myself, nobody will expect me to demur.[1] It shows further that the 'something about it' must be something thought desirable, or thought to be a means to something desirable. I do not think that I want to object to this either, provided that 'desire' and 'desirable' are taken in fairly wide senses, as translations of the Aristotelian *orexis* and *orekton*. So interpreted, the argument shows that, whenever we think something good, it must be, or be thought by us to be a means to, something to 'try to get'[2] which (in actual or hypothetical circumstances) we have at least some disposition. This conclusion, which has, it may be noticed, marked non-descriptivist undertones, is one I can agree with. The crucial thing to notice, however, is that the argument does nothing to show what may

[1] *FR*, p. 71; *LM*, p. 133.
[2] See Anscombe, op. cit., p. 67; *FR*, p. 70.

or may not be the subject of a desirability characterisation. It could, so far as this way of taking the argument goes, be anything you please. Thus, if our desires concerning wines were different, which they logically could be, 'tasting ϕ' might be an '*un*-desirability characterisation'; and we should not be in the least put out if we found a man who wanted *not* to drink Colombey 1972 because it tasted like that.

The second way of taking the expression 'desirability characterisation' is as follows: we give a desirability characterisation of an object if we say something about it which is *logically* tied in some way (weak or strong) to desiring. An example of this would be to say that something would be fun; others would be to call it pleasant, or interesting, or delightful. Notice that, in this sense of 'desirability characterisation', to say that the wine tasted ϕ would *not* be to give a desirability characterisation of it; for there is no logical connexion between thinking that a thing tastes ϕ and desiring it. As I have said, a man might without logical fault say that he wanted *not* to drink Colombey 1972 because it tasted ϕ; and he might also say something less committal, namely that the fact that it tasted ϕ did not make him either want to drink it or want not to drink it – in short that he was indifferent to its tasting ϕ. But it would be logically odd for somebody to say that the fact that something would be pleasant, or fun, or interesting, or delightful, did not make him – to the smallest degree – disposed to do it (though of course he might not be disposed to do it when he considered the whole situation, including its consequences and the alternatives).

It may be that there is also a connexion in the reverse direction between being fun, etc., and being desired or thought good; though, if so, the nature of the connexion is obscure and tenuous. It may be, that is to say, that if we have said that we want something, or that we think it good, it is natural for us, if asked why, to say that it would be fun, or pleasant, or to give it some other characterisation falling within an ill-defined class which includes these. It may even be true that it is logically compulsory, on pain of making ourselves incomprehensible, that we should be prepared to give such an explanation.

The difficulty with this suggestion is that it is not possible to rule out, *a priori*, additions to the list of desirability characterisations in this second sense. And it is a somewhat vacuous claim that an explanation falling within a certain class must be forthcoming, if the class itself is so easily expansible. 'Exciting' is a desirability characterisation – and in at least some uses a desirability characterisation in the second of my two senses. Let us suppose, then, that there is a race of men who have not, up till now, valued the experience of danger (perhaps because their conditions of life have been such as to give them altogether too much of it), and have therefore not had the favourable characterisation 'exciting' in their vocabulary, but only such unfavourable characterisations as 'frightening' and 'terrifying'. Then, when their life becomes less exposed to terrors, they begin to know what it is to be bored, and so come to value excitement for its own sake. There then comes to be a need for the favourable characterisation 'exciting', and they duly invent it. This is an example of what I mean by an addition to the list of desirability characterisations in the second sense.

One reason why it is easy to be confused by these two possible senses of the phrase 'desirability characterisation' is that words which are very commonly used as desirability characterisations in the first sense often end up by becoming desirability characterisations in the second sense. That is to say, they acquire a logical, as opposed to a merely contingent, connexion with being desired. The Latin word *virtus* underwent such a shift, owing to the contingent fact that the properties which are typical of the male sex are properties which the Romans desired people to have. Thus in particular cases it is sometimes hard to say whether a word is being used as a desirability characterisation in the second sense. But this will not cause concern to anybody unless he is a victim of the 'heap' fallacy to which I referred earlier.

A confusion between the two senses of 'desirability characterisation' might lead a careless descriptivist to suppose that descriptivism could be established in the following way. We should first establish that anything that is thought good must also be thought to be the subject of some desirability characterisation, or a means to such (and here it does not matter for the argument in which sense the phrase is used; let us allow for the sake of argument that this premiss is true in both senses). We should then point out (correctly) that only some *words* can be desirability characterisations (sense two). Then we should assume that this proved that only some *things* can be the subjects of desirability characterisations (sense one). And so we should think that we had proved that only some things can be thought good. But the two connected fallacies in this argument should by now be obvious. The first is the equivocation on the phrase 'desirability characterisation'. The second is the assumption that by proving that there are certain words that cannot be or that must be used in conjunction with the statement that something is good, we have proved that certain things cannot be thought good.

It must always be possible to want, or to think good, *new* sorts of thing (for example, new experiences); and therefore it can never be nonsense to *say* that we want them, or that they are good, provided that we are careful not to describe them in a way which is logically inconsistent with this. It is said that under the influence of mescaline people say things like 'How simply marvellous that at the corner of the room three planes meet at a point!' So perhaps they might, on occasion, say (to use Miss Anscombe's example) 'How simply marvellous to have this saucer of mud!' And if somebody asks what is marvellous about it, why should they not reply, with respectable precedent, 'We can't tell you; you have to have the experience before any word for it would mean anything to you:

Nec lingua valet dicere,
Nec litera exprimere;
Expertus potest credere' ?

It may readily be admitted that whenever we desire something, it must be because of something about it; but if pressed to say what this something is, we may be tempted, since most of my opponents on this question are of the opposite sex, to rejoin with Wilbye's madrigal:

Love me not for comely grace,
For my pleasing eye or face,
Nor for any outward part;
No, nor for my constant heart;
For those may fail or turn to ill,
So thou and I shall sever.
Keep therefore a true woman's eye,
And love me still, but know not why,
So hast thou the same reason still
To dote upon me ever.

Note that the poet does not here say that there is *no* reason for a woman's loving, but that she does not have to know (in the sense of 'know how to say') what it is.

That logic cannot determine what we are going to be attracted by or averse from was well known to Shakespeare. He makes Shylock say, when challenged as to his motives for demanding the pound of flesh,

> Some men there are love not a gaping pig;
> Some, that are mad if they behold a cat;
> And others, when the bag-pipe sings i' th' nose,
> Cannot contain their urine; for affection,
> Mistress of passion, sways it to the mood
> Of what it likes or loaths.   (*M. of V.* IV i)

And he knew about love-potions, of one of which he says,

> The juice of it, on sleeping eyelids laid,
> Will make or man or woman madly dote
> Upon the next live creature that it sees . . .
> The next thing then she waking looks upon,
> (Be it on lion, bear, or wolf, or bull,
> On meddling monkey, or on busy ape,)
> She shall pursue it with the soul of love.
> (M.N.D. II i)

There are no logical limits (at least none relevant to the present issue)[1] to what such potions could make even a descriptivist philosopher desire; and therefore, if an argument about what can (logically) be thought good is based upon what can (logically) be desired, it is bound to fail. Logic tells us, indeed, that, if a man claims to desire a certain thing, there are certain *words* which he must not apply to it, and perhaps also that there are certain other words, some of which at least he must be prepared to apply to it. But the latter half of this logical restriction is rather indefinite and elusive, and I leave it to those who have a stake in it to make it more determinate than it is so far. The trouble is that, as Miss Anscombe rightly says, *bonum est multiplex*; and I can see no way of putting a logical limit to its multiplicity.

---

[1] For some restrictions which, though interesting, do not affect the present argument, see Anscombe, op. cit., p. 66 and A. Kenny, *Action, Emotion and Will*, p. 112. Since states of affairs can be desired for their own sakes, the restriction that what is desired must be desired *for* something is a vacuous one.

VI

The point that I have been making – or a closely related point
– can be put in the following way. We can perhaps distinguish
between objective properties of objects – i.e. those which they
have, however a person is disposed towards them – and subjective properties, which an object has only if a person is disposed towards it in a certain way. I must confess that I do not
like these words, because they have been used in too many
different senses; but perhaps, as so defined, they will serve our
present purposes. In a similar way, we might distinguish between objective conditions which have to be satisfied before we
can use a certain word of an object, and subjective conditions.
The former consist in the possession by the object of objective
properties; the latter in a person's being disposed in a certain
way towards it. Now descriptivists often seem to be wanting to
demonstrate to us that there are certain objective conditions
for the use of words like 'good'. But the most that arguments
like the foregoing can show is that there are certain subjective
conditions.

Here, moreover, we must guard against another, related,
ambiguity in the expression 'conditions for the use of a word'.
It might mean 'conditions for a word being said to be used
correctly to express what the speaker who calls a thing "good"
(for example) is wishing to convey'; or it might mean 'conditions for a thing's being said to be good'. This ambiguity is well
illustrated on the first page of an article by Mrs Foot.[1] In
outlining a position which she is going to attack, she asks: 'Is a
connexion with the choices of the speaker ever a *sufficient* condition for the use of the word "good", as it would be if a man
could ever call certain things (let us call them *A*s) good *A*s
simply because these were the *A*s which he was thereafter ready
to choose?' She goes on to argue that it is neither a sufficient nor
a necessary condition; in this she deviates from Miss Anscombe,
who thinks that if we call a thing good, we must attribute to it
some desirability characteristic, and that 'the primitive sign of
wanting is trying to get'.[2]

Now if here 'a sufficient condition for the use of the word
"good"' meant 'a sufficient condition for a thing's being said

[1] *Ar. Soc. Supp.*, xxxv (1961) 45.
[2] Op. cit., p. 67; see above, p. 63.

to be good', then it is, I think, quite plain that a connexion with choices is not a sufficient condition. At any rate, I have never thought that it was; indeed, though the view has sometimes been attributed to me that 'So and so is a good *x*' means the same as 'So and so is the *x* (or kind of *x*) that I would choose', this is a position which I have explicitly argued against.[1] Now there are indications in the article which might lead one to suppose that Mrs Foot was taking the words 'sufficient condition for the use of the word "good"' to mean 'sufficient condition for a thing's being said to be good'. The chief indication is that few if any of her arguments are even plausible unless this were what she was trying to disprove. Also, her words in several places naturally bear this sense. For example, on p. 53 she says (referring to an example of a person playing a game with pebbles) 'It is not by his readiness to pick up the pebbles that he *legitimizes his words*'; and she has just said that, on the contrary, 'It is a plain matter of fact that the particular *A*s' (in this example pebbles) '*will be* good for his purposes, or from his point of view' (my italics). A similar kind of expression occurs earlier on p. 46, where she says, of a man talking about knives, 'He could not say that a good knife was one which rusted quickly, *defending his use* of the word "good" by showing that he picked out such knives for his own use.' It certainly looks, at first sight, as if in both these instances, by 'legitimize his words' and 'defend his use' she means, not 'show that he really does think that sort of knife or pebble good, and is therefore expressing correctly what he thinks', but rather 'show that the knives or pebbles which he calls good *are* good'. So it looked to me, when I first read the article, as if, when she was constructing these arguments, she had the purpose of attacking a position which I, at any rate, have never defended, and with which, therefore, I need not concern myself.

However, we must consider the other possible interpretation, in view of the fact that, unless my memory is deceiving me, and my notes incorrect (and I am not confident on either point), this was the interpretation which she authorised at the meeting at which her paper was discussed, after I had pointed out to her that on the first interpretation she was attacking a position which was not mine. If this second interpretation were what she meant, then in the 'pebble' example she would be maintaining

[1] *LM*, p. 107.

that, if a man were ready to pick up a certain kind of pebble for playing a game, and habitually did so, to point this out would not be a way of showing that those were the pebbles that he thought good for his purposes or from his point of view, and thus 'legitimizing' the use of the word 'good' by showing that it correctly expressed his thought (however preposterous the thought). But if so, she was maintaining something that is not very plausible. For if a man consistently and deliberately chose a certain kind of pebble, we *should* infer that he thought that kind of pebble good for his purposes or from his point of view; if we had doubts, they would be about what on earth the purposes or the point of view could be. I conclude that either she was attacking a position which I have never held, or else she was attacking one which I might, with certain explanations, accept, but attacking it in a way which could carry conviction only to somebody who confused the two possible interpretations of the phrase 'condition for'.

VII

This seems to be the best point at which to deal with another common descriptivist manœuvre. The manœuvre is rendered attractive by the following fact, which I think we can all admit. There are some things which, if wanted or thought good by somebody, seem to call for no explanation (for example, food, a certain degree of warmth, etc.). Other things, if wanted or thought good, require explanation. The explanation can perhaps be given: a man who wants a flat pebble may want it to play ducks and drakes with, and think it good for this purpose; but, as we progress to more and more bizarre examples, the explanation gets harder and harder to give. It therefore seems to be open to the descriptivist to take a very extraordinary imaginary example, and ask rhetorical questions about it, such as 'Suppose that a man says that somebody is a good man because he clasps and unclasps his hands, and never turns NNE. after turning SSW.; could we understand him?'[1] It is implied that an anti-descriptivist has to claim that he can understand such an absurd statement, and this is treated as a *reductio ad absurdum* of his position.

[1] The example comes from Mrs Foot's article in *Ar. Soc.*, LIX (1958–9) 84.

This type of argument rests on a confusion between, on the one hand, logical absurdity and its various weaker analogues, and, on the other, various sorts of contingent improbability. That is why I said earlier that the problem about the distinction between descriptive and evaluative is an offshoot of the problem about the distinction between analytic and synthetic. It is contingently extremely unlikely, to say the least, that I should become able to lift a ton weight with my bare hands; but it is not logically impossible for this to happen, nor is it logically absurd, in any weaker way, to claim that it has happened. By this I mean that if a man claimed to be able to do this, there would be no ultimate obstacle to our understanding him. Admittedly, we might well think at first that we had misunderstood him; it is so improbable that anybody should even think that it had happened, that, if a person claimed that it had happened, we should think at first that he could not be meaning the words in their literal senses. We might think that he meant, for instance, that the weight in question was counter-balanced, so that he could put his hands underneath it and lift, and make it go up. That is to say, when a man says something which is sufficiently improbable (as we think the universe to be constituted), we tend to assume that he cannot mean it literally, and that therefore we have to search for some non-literal meaning if we are going to understand him. But for all that, what he says has in its literal sense nothing *logically* wrong with it. It follows that no conclusions whatever are to be drawn concerning the meanings or uses of words from the oddity of such a remark; what is odd is not the use of words, but that anybody should think such a thing.

The case before us is much the same. If a man said that somebody was a good man because he clasped and unclasped his hands, we should, indeed, at first find ourselves wondering whether we had understood him. But the reason is that, although what has been said is perfectly *comprehensible* in its literal sense, it is very odd indeed for anybody to think it. We should therefore look around for non-literal senses or contrived explanations, and should be baffled if we failed to find any. Why would it be odd for anybody to think this? For a reason which can, indeed, be gathered from the writings of descriptivists, who have given a tolerably correct account of it, vitiated only by their assumption that it can teach us anything about the uses or meanings of words, and that therefore it can support, or discredit, logical theses. The reason is that very few of us, if any, have the necessary 'pro-attitude' to people who clasp and unclasp their hands; and the reason for this is that the pro-attitudes which we have do not just occur at random, but have explanations, albeit not (as the descriptivists whom I am discussing seem to think) explanations which logic alone could provide. To think something good of its kind is, let us say, to have at least some disposition to choose it when, or if, choosing things of that kind, in actual or hypothetical circumstances. After what I have said earlier, you will not, I know, confuse this thesis with the thesis that for something to *be* good is for us to have a disposition to choose it. Now we do not have, most of us, any disposition to choose, or to choose to be, men who clasp and unclasp their hands. We do not, accordingly, think that men who do this are good.

The explanation of our not thinking this is that such choices would hardly contribute to our survival, growth, procreation, etc.; if there have been any races of men or animals who have made the clasping and unclasping of hands a prime object of their pro-attitudes, to the exclusion of other more survival-promoting activities, they have gone under in the struggle for existence. I am, I know, being rather crude; but in general, to cut the matter short, we have the pro-attitudes that we have, and therefore call the things good which we do call good, because of their relevance to certain ends which are sometimes called 'fundamental human needs'.

To call them this, however, is already to make a *logical* connexion between them and what it is good for a man to have. This, indeed, is why descriptivists have fallen into the trap of supposing that, because the word 'good' is logically tied in certain contexts to the *word* 'needs', it is therefore logically tied to certain concrete *things* which are generally thought to be needs. But since this mistake is the same mistake as I discussed at length in connexion with desires, it need not detain us. The two words 'desires' and 'needs' have both misled descriptivists in the same way – and that because there is an intimate logical relation between what is needed and what is desired, so that in many contexts we could say that for a thing to be needed is for it to be a necessary condition for satisfying a desire. It follows that if 'things desired' do not form a closed class, 'things needed' will not either. If, as I said, logic does not prevent us from coming to desire new things, or ceasing to desire old ones, it cannot, either, determine what we do or do not need.

A man who used the word 'good' of things which were unrelated to those ends which most of us call 'needs' might, nevertheless, be using it, quite correctly, to express the thought which he had; but this might be (if a sufficiently crazy example were taken) a very extraordinary thought for a man to have, because most of us have a high regard for our survival, and for such other things as I mentioned, and our pro-attitudes are fairly consistently related to these. It is not, indeed, logically necessary that they should be. Those of some people are not. And it would not affect my argument (though it would obviously affect gravely that of the opposite party) if there were some things which some people just do, unaccountably, have a high regard for, like the music of Beethoven.

In short, our disposition to call only a certain range of things good (and to choose and desire them) can be explained – in so far as it can be explained – without bringing in logic; and therefore the explanation contributes nothing to logic either, and, specifically, tells us nothing about the meanings or uses of he evaluative words, except that they have certain common *descriptive* meanings.

VIII

I shall end this lecture with an attempt to clear up a quite simple confusion about the word 'because' – a confusion which seems to me to lie at the root of a great many things which descriptivists say. If I am choosing between an ordinary mushroom and a poisonous toadstool to put in the dish that I am making for myself, I naturally choose, and prefer, and think it best to choose and that I ought to choose, the mushroom and not the toadstool; and I think this *because* the latter is poisonous (i.e. such as to cause death if eaten). That the toadstool is poisonous is my *reason* for rejecting it. Now it might be thought that, if I reject it *because* it is poisonous, there must be some logical connexion between the statement 'It is poisonous' and the statements 'It ought not to be chosen to eat' or 'It is not good to eat'; or between my thought that it is poisonous and my disposition not to eat it. By 'logical connexion' I mean that the *meanings* of the expressions are somehow linked (the precise nature of the link need not concern us; some descriptivists would make it a firmer one than others). Now to say this is to confuse logical entailment, together with its many weaker analogues, on the one hand, with the relation between choice and reasons for choice on the other. The relation between choice and reasons for choice is not a logical relation. There is no logical compulsion on me, or even any weaker logical constraint, to refrain from eating what I know will kill me. I refrain from eating it *because* I know it will kill me; but if I did the opposite, and *ate* it because I knew it would kill me, I should not be offending against any logical rule regulating the uses of words, however fashionably tenuous the rule is supposed to be.

There is, indeed, a logical inference that can be elicited from this situation. Given that the toadstool would kill me, I can infer that I ought not to eat it, if I also accept a further premiss that I ought not to eat what would kill me. To accept this other premiss is to have one of a class of things which I shall call, in Professor Braithwaite's phrase, 'springs of action'.[1] Desires belong to this class, as do convictions that something is better than something else. In fact anything belongs to it which can, as it were, turn a descriptive statement into a reason for doing something; or, more formally, the expression of which in language (though not, of course, its *description* in language), together with some descriptive statement, logically entails some prescription. But there is no logical link between the descriptive premiss, *by itself*, and the prescriptive conclusion.

A parallel from a quite distinct field of discourse, which has nothing to do with prescriptions, will perhaps make this point clear. There is a valid logical inference from the statement that cyanide is a poison, together with the statement that this dish contains cyanide, to the conclusion that this dish contains poison. But there is no logical connexion which can justify the inference from the statement, by itself, that the dish contains cyanide, to the conclusion that it contains poison. This is because the other premiss, that cyanide is a poison, is synthetic. Nevertheless, the dish is poisonous *because* it contains cyanide.

Now if anybody thinks that one can never say '*q* because *p*' unless there is a logical connexion between '*p*' and '*q*', he is

---

[1] *Ar. Soc. Supp.*, xx (1946) 9. Aristotle's *orexeis* and Kenny's 'volitions' (op. cit., p. 214) play similar roles.

likely to attempt to place opponents of descriptivism in the following dilemma. Either we have to admit that there is a logical connexion between statements of fact, taken by themselves, and evaluative conclusions (which is to surrender to at any rate a weak form of descriptivism); or else we must hold that evaluative judgements are never made *because* of anything – i.e. that they are quite irrational. It is to be hoped that if descriptivists reflect upon the falsity of this dilemma, they will abandon at least some of their arguments.

This lecture has been polemical. I felt it necessary to discuss certain mistaken views (as I think them to be); for it seems to me that, if we could put them behind us, we might liberate the subject for a real advance. In this sense my lecture has had a constructive purpose.

6 Pain and Evil

1. It has been held by some philosophers in the past that pain is not an evil, or not necessarily so.[1] In contrast with these ancient opinions, we find some modern philosophers maintaining, not merely that pain *is* an evil – an opinion with which most of us would agree – but that this, or something like this, is true in virtue of the very meaning of the word 'pain', and that it is therefore logically absurd to deny it. In this paper I shall be concerned less with the question of whether pain is, analytically, an evil, than with the preliminary questions of whether it is logically possible to experience pain but not dislike it, whether pain logically entails suffering, and the like. I shall leave undiscussed the precise relations between disliking something and thinking of it as an evil, and between being caused to suffer and undergoing an evil.

It must be noted, also, that the following sorts of cases are irrelevant to the questions which I shall be discussing:

(1) Cases in which a person does not notice or attend to a pain which he feels (or which he would feel if he attended to it) because he is concentrating on something else (e.g., the game of football he is playing);

(2) Cases in which a person, though he dislikes, in itself, the pain which he has, accepts it willingly as a necessary condition for attaining something else which he values (e.g., sexual satisfaction or the purgation of sin). It has been suggested that the masochist falls into this class; I am not sure about this, but I shall for this reason leave him out.*

Reprinted from *Aristotelian Society Supplement*, xxxviii (1964). © The Aristotelian Society 1964.

[1] See, e.g., M. Antoninus, vi 33.

* Mr Gardiner, in his contribution to the same symposium, made some interesting observations on this topic.

That is to say, I shall be discussing the question whether it is possible for a person not to dislike *in itself* (or, analogously, not to be caused to suffer, *pro tanto*, by) a pain to which he gives his full attention.

2. I will take, as an example of the thesis that pain has, analytically, to be disliked, the view of Professor Baier.[1] Baier's view is expounded by way of dissent from a statement of Professor Ryle's that 'Pain is a sensation of a special sort, which we ordinarily dislike having'.[2] Baier rejects the word 'ordinarily', as implying contingency. He thinks that the fact that we dislike pains is not a contingent fact; 'whatever sorts of sensations we like and dislike, we only call pains those which we dislike. And if there are sensations which we ordinarily dislike but on some occasions like having, then we do not call them pains on those occasions on which we like having them.'[3]

It is not clear from what Baier says whether he thinks that there is a distinct sensation or group of sensations called 'pain', different from, e.g., warmth, cold and pressure, or whether he thinks that 'pain' is simply a word we use of *any* sensation when, either because it has reached a certain intensity, or for some other reason, we dislike it. If he thinks the former, it will be difficult for him to answer the question, what we call this distinct sensation on those occasions, which he admits to exist, when we do not dislike it (since the description 'pain' is ruled out by his theory). If there is this distinct sensation, there is surely a place for a word to describe it without entailing dislike.[4] It is conceivable, indeed, that, since we almost universally dislike the sensation in question, we have not developed any word at all for describing it without implying

---

[1] *The Moral Point of View*, pp. 268 ff.

[2] *The Concept of Mind*, p. 109.

[3] Op. cit., p. 273.

[4] We shall see later that there are some narrower words (sometimes metaphorical) like 'pricking' and 'stinging' which are used of certain kinds of sensation which are certainly called 'pain' when they are intense enough to be disliked, but which there is a temptation to call 'pain' even when not disliked. These words, however, cannot be what we are looking for, since they would be inappropriate to other kinds of pain (e.g. pain caused by cold). On Baier's theory, interpreted in this first way, there ought to be a general word for the sensation which when we dislike it we call 'pain', but a word which can also be applied to it when we do not dislike it.

dislike; but it is much more likely that we merely have not developed any *separate* word – i.e., that the word 'pain' itself is sometimes used to refer neutrally to this bare sensation, though sometimes, as no doubt Ryle also would admit, it is used in such a way as to imply dislike. If this were so, the controversy between Baier and Ryle would begin to wear thin; for they might both be giving more or less correct accounts of different uses of the word 'pain'.

Baier's account, however, suffers more from ambiguity than Ryle's does; for we still have to consider the possibility that Baier thinks that there is no *distinct* sensation called 'pain', but that 'pain' is simply the name we give to any sensation when we dislike it. This view is less plausible. It has to meet the question of why, in that case, we do not call itches 'pains' – or sweltering heat, or cramps, or electric shocks, or the sensations which we have when tickled, or which we can give ourselves by gently massaging the funny bone, or by scraping our finger-nails down a blackboard. I must confess that the more I think about this subject, the more unpleasant sensations I seem to identify in my experience which are not pains. We have a phrase for the whole genus of these sensations, namely, 'unpleasant sensation'; but 'pain' seems to be a far narrower word than this.

It is true that often, when some sensation other than pain (e.g., warmth) becomes sufficiently intense, we start to feel pain; and it might be claimed that 'pain' means not '*any* disliked sensation' but, more narrowly, 'any of a limited number of sensations – including warmth, cold and pressure – when disliked because above a certain intensity'. But even this will not do. For when we are touching something that is getting hotter, and the sensation of warmth turns to one of pain, and we say 'Now the sensation is painful', we do not mean the same as we would if we said that the sensation of warmth had got so intense that we disliked it. Neither logically nor phenomenologically is pain merely the upper end of the scales of intensity of the other sensations, coupled with dislike.

It seems, rather, that there is a phenomenologically distinct sensation or group of sensations which we have when we are in pain, and that there could be (whether there actually is or not) a word for this group of sensations which did not imply dislike. I say 'group of sensations' because burning pains, stinging pains, stabbing pains, aches, etc., are distinguishable from one another, although they clearly fall into a group which is bound together by more than the fact that they are all disliked. This phenomenologically distinct group of sensations, however, is almost universally disliked, and therefore it is convenient for us to have a word (such as 'pain' almost certainly is in one of its uses) which does imply dislike, but also is confined to this distinct group of sensations, and cannot be used of, for example, electric shocks, itches or tickles. There is also a place for more general words or phrases which imply dislike, but are not restricted as to the sensation which is the object of the dislike. 'Unpleasant sensation' seems to be a phrase of this kind. Itches, tickles, electric shocks, etc., are unpleasant sensations, but they are not pains.

There are thus, in principle, at least three categories of words which we might use in speaking of our experiences when we are in pain. Our actual words may be expected to overflow from one of these categories into another, so that we shall often have to say that in one use a word falls into one category, while in another use it falls into a different category. This should not dismay us. The three categories are:

(1) Words which refer simply to the bare sensation, without implying dislike. I think that 'pain', in one of its uses, falls into this category, and would be so used more often if the occasions on which we have the sensation without disliking it were not so uncommon. This would seem to be the sense of the word to which Ryle refers.

(2) Words which refer to this same sensation, but in addition imply dislike, so that they cannot be used when the sensation is had but not disliked. If we used 'pain$_1$' and 'pain$_2$' for the word as used in the first and second categories respectively, we might say, without much distortion, that 'pain$_2$' meant 'pain$_1$ which is disliked' or 'pain$_1$ which is unpleasant'. 'Agony' and 'anguish' seem, in their literal senses, to fall into this category. If we speak of the 'agony' of a person who is not suffering intensely on account of one of the distinct group of sensations called 'pain', we do so in a metaphorical sense. The verb 'hurt' (intransitive), like 'pain' itself, seems to be used in both these first two categories, and, indeed, metaphorically in the third.

(3) Words which imply dislike, but can also be used of other things than pain in the literal sense. Such words are

'suffering', 'unpleasant', 'distress', and 'discomfort'. There will also, as we have seen, be found in this category metaphorical uses of words whose literal habitat is in one of the first two categories or both. For example, an unkind remark can hurt me.

3. Objection might be taken to the claim that there could be a 'bare sensation' of pain which was not disliked. What, it might be asked, would such an experience be like? Can we *imagine* such an experience? I think that I can not only imagine it, but have had it; but I shall return to this question later. Here I shall just make the obvious point that we cannot conclude, from the fact that something surpasses our imagination, that it cannot happen. I cannot myself imagine what the electric torture would be like; but that does not take away the possibility that it might be inflicted on me. It would be more relevant if it could be established that no *sense* could be given to the expression 'experience which is like pain except for not being disliked'. But that is precisely the question at issue, and this whole paper is an attempt to see what sense can be given to such an expression.

An analogy may help us to understand this question. Let us suppose that I have always disliked a certain degree of cold (for example, that which I experience when I dive into water of a certain temperature having up till then been lying in the shade in still air of a certain other temperature; the experimental conditions could be made more exact, but this will be enough for our purposes). I am assuming that the coldness of the water is not sufficient to produce actual pain. Now is it not perfectly possible to understand what it would be like for me to experience the same degree of cold, but not dislike it (not be caused any discomfort or distress)? Suppose, for example, that I do this diving act many times in the hope of getting not to mind this degree of cold; and that in the end I succeed. It is not necessary to suppose that there is any change in the degree of cold that I feel (even subjectively); there might be, but that would spoil the example. It may be merely that through habituation I stop minding my skin feeling like that. We do not even need to suppose any course of habituation. Whether I found the cold unpleasant or invigorating might depend on my general state of mind – on whether I was feeling depressed or elated.

In the case of cold, the vocabulary which we actually have

contains an expression – 'to feel cold' – which does not imply
dislike. Even in the case of cold, admittedly, dislike of the
sensation above a certain intensity is so universal that it might
be assumed that a person who said he felt cold *did* dislike it,
although the word itself does not imply this. But nevertheless,
'I liked feeling cold' is perfectly comprehensible. Intense cold
can be liked because invigorating – and this does not mean 'as a
means to the end of being invigorated'. *A fortiori*, it can be not
disliked. But our vocabulary might have been different – it is
very important to distinguish the question 'What does our
present vocabulary allow?' from the question 'How could it
comprehensibly be modified?' We could, that is to say, have
had a word for the feeling of cold which did, like 'pain' in some
of its uses, imply dislike. Let us suppose that 'cold' itself was
used in this way, and that dislike of cold was much more
universal than in fact it is, so that uses of 'cold' in the other way,
as not implying dislike, were comparatively rare. 'Cold' would
then behave much as 'pain' does now, in respect of implying or
not implying dislike (though, of course, there would be other
differences).

The difference between the behaviour of our *actual* words
'cold' and 'pain' reflects a difference in how people commonly
react to these two sensations; but – and this is really the nub –
that does not mean that we are under any *logical* constraint to
react to cold or pain in the way that we do. The constraints that
we are under are contingent, though they too are readily
explicable. There are good reasons why very few people get into
a state in which they do not mind high intensities of pain.
Nearly all causes of pain are also causes of harm to the organism;
pain is, therefore, such a good warning device – and has indeed
been developed as such – that we have acquired, partly by
evolution and partly by learning, a very firm disposition to
avoid pain; and this firm disposition is associated with a subjective feeling of dislike. This dislike is so universal that it is,
as we have seen, reflected in our vocabulary; but that does not
make it anything else but contingent that we have the dislike –
there logically could be a person who did not dislike high intensities of the sensation. With our vocabulary as it is, he could
say that he did not dislike the pain, using the word in the
sense of 'pain' above; but unless such cases became common,
there would certainly be conceptual misunderstandings and

difficulties owing to the possibility of confusion between the two senses of the word which I have labelled 'pain$_1$' and 'pain$_2$'. And this is what has actually happened in the experimental and clinical situations to which I shall refer below.

The reasons why our actual word 'cold' does not behave like our actual word 'pain', in the sense of 'pain$_2$', are readily understandable. People who do not mind, or who like, high intensities of cold, though uncommon, are not *so* uncommon. Probably nobody who breaks the ice to bathe at Christmas and enjoys it does so without a good deal of self-schooling; but we all know perfectly well that the thing can be done. With 'pain' it would be much more of an oddity. I have said that I would leave the masochist out, because there is a doubt whether his case is relevant. We must therefore look for clearer cases. There are, in fact, small degrees of pain which are by no means disliked by everybody. Most people could draw the point of a needle rather gently across their skin (as in acupuncture) and say truthfully that they could distinctly feel pain, but that they did not dislike it. Some might say that they would rather be without it than with it; but that would apply to a great many sensations about which no philosopher, to my knowledge, takes the line that some do with pain. Most people would rather be without a feeling of giddiness (though children often induce it in themselves out of interest); but nobody says that no sense can be given to the sentence 'I feel giddy, but do not dislike it'.

With some diffidence in the use of this technical term, we might say that the 'threshold' of dislike of pain is usually somewhat above the threshold of pain itself (that is, of the pain$_1$-sensation).[1] Now let us suppose that we have a pain which is only just above the threshold of dislike. May I not, by habituation, come *not* to dislike this – to raise the threshold of dislike? We do not, perhaps, have to be heroes to achieve this much. But in any case, it is not necessary actually to achieve it. It is sufficient – indeed more than sufficient – to imagine what it would be like to achieve it; and this I find perfectly easy. Indeed, even imagination is, for the reason given above, not

---

[1] See C. A. Keele, in *The Assessment of Pain in Man and Animals*, ed. Keele and Smith (1962) p. 41. Many of the other papers in this symposium are of considerable philosophical interest, especially that by R. Smith. I return to Keele's work below.

necessary. It is sufficient if I could understand what would be meant by somebody who claimed to have achieved this very minor feat. And this I can certainly do. But if I can do it in this marginal case, I do not see how it can be impossible to *understand*, though it may be difficult to *believe*, a man who says that, by practice, he has got into a state in which he does not dislike lying on a bed of nails, although he has exactly the same experiences, apart from the dislike, that I would have if I lay on a bed of nails. The case is analogous to that of a man who claims to be able to jump, unaided, twenty feet into the air, whereas I can jump only three feet into the air. I understand him, but I do not readily believe him. That in the 'bed of nails' case there would be a logical bar to demonstrating conclusively that the feat had been performed (he might just be *very* good at concealing his dislike) does not seem to me to be relevant.

I have put this whole argument in terms of the word 'dislike'. I think that it could have been put equally well in terms of the word 'discomfort', or 'suffering', or 'unpleasant'. I have heard it said that it is logically impossible for a man who is experiencing intense pain not to be suffering, because suffering just *is* intense pain. This is clearly wrong, not only for the irrelevant reason that there are other ways of suffering than by experiencing intense pain (tickling or stifling, for example, will do); but because, by an analogous argument to the preceding, it would become clear that we could understand my *faqir* on his bed of nails if he said that he was experiencing intense pain, but not suffering, not finding it unpleasant, and undergoing no discomfort.

4. I have discussed the problem so far with reference to our common experience. While looking for more exact accounts of the distinction between pain, considered as a bare sensation, and pain, considered as entailing dislike, I have read a good deal of physiological literature, though not, I fear, enough to be sure that I have understood the very difficult physiological issues about which there is at the moment so much controversy going on. I will, however, select two physiological topics which I think have a very close bearing on our philosophical problem, and do my best to summarise what the physiologists say about them.

An attempt has been made, which is of great philosophical

interest, to record the precise verbal descriptions given by experimental subjects of their experience when subjected to varying amounts of pain.[1] These verbal descriptions can be supplemented by one physiologist's account of his own experiences, and what he is disposed to say about them, and also by the records of the movements of an indicator moved by the subjects to correspond with their subjective experiences. The indicator scale was marked 'No pain: slight: moderate: severe: very severe.'

Two contrasting features are very noticeable in the reports of these experiments. The first is a definite tendency, which supports the view of Baier, for subjects to confine the description 'pain' to experiences which they found unpleasant. For sensations (induced by putting various chemicals on an exposed blister base) which were not so intense as to be unpleasant, they used words like 'stinging' and 'pricking' (Smith, pp. 38–40). The other feature, which, on the contrary, supports Ryle's view, is the suggestion that the quality of the sensation below the level of unpleasantness is 'continuous in most ways' with that above; Keele (p. 30) says, 'the element of unpleasantness seems to be superimposed on a sensation which runs through the whole range'. The 'continuity' of the sensation was to some extent borne out (for anyone but a philosopher) by the fact that, when the movements of the indicator recording the subjective intensity of the sensation were plotted against the amounts of the chemical in the solution applied to the blister (on a logarithmic scale), a very good correlation resulted.

Keele, attacking the conceptual difficulty in what seems a very sensible way, says, 'It is simplest . . . to speak of a sensation of cutaneous pain which may range from the barest detectable level' (he has said earlier, on p. 30, that the sensation may be neutral or even pleasing) 'to an intolerably unpleasant experience. If the word pain is used to characterise this sensation throughout its whole scale it would be convenient to have some qualifying word to describe that part of the scale in which the sensation is usually not unpleasant. Phrases such as "non-painful pain" and "sub-threshold pain" are clearly not applicable.' He proposes the technical terms 'metaesthesia' for the lower part of the scale and 'algaesthesia' for the higher, unpleasant part. Some such technical vocabulary is obviously

[1] C. A. Keele and R. Smith, op. cit.

required, since the ordinary word 'pain' has given rise to confusion because of its ambiguity, already noticed. Keele goes on:
'It must, however, be emphasised that the borderline between
the metaesthetic and algaesthetic ranges of pain is variable and
hard to define, but of the reality of the distinction between these
two ranges of pain there can be no doubt.'

While, as philosophers, we might cavil at some of this, I think
that we should be content with the broad lines of this suggestion.
The upshot is that there are two ranges of intensity of a certain
sensation, the boundary between which is indefinite and
variable; there is a tendency, but only a tendency, in ordinary
subjects to reserve the word 'pain' for the higher, unpleasant,
range, but an opposing tendency, stronger among the experi-
menters themselves, but perfectly comprehensible to anyone,
to use the word 'pain' of the whole range, pleasant, neutral or
unpleasant. Once the phenomena are recognised – as they
perhaps cannot be without more careful attention than the
average man or even the average philosopher gives to the
matter – we do not need to attach too much importance to the
terminology, provided that it is consistently used; we shall have
no difficulty in describing the phenomena whichever terminology we adopt.

5. The other physiological topic which I think it worth while
to introduce (though with the greatest diffidence) is that of
lobotomy. There is, as is well known, an operation to the frontal
lobes of the brain which markedly alters what physiologists and
psychologists call the 'pain-reaction'. Unfortunately this term is
highly ambiguous, and before we can discuss the effects of the
operation we shall have to sort out its different senses. We may
distinguish, within the general class of reactions to pain, the
following:

(1) Experiences:
    (a) The felt dislike of the pain;
    (b) The felt desire to be rid of the pain; some people
        might equate this with (a);
    (c) The felt desire or inclination to do some particular
        thing in order to be rid of the pain: e.g., to try to
        prevent the surgeon moving a painful limb;
    (d) Various after-effects such as fear of the painful event
        happening again.

(2) Behaviour:
    (e) Various automatic reactions or reflexes such as wincing, crying out, etc. We do not need to discuss whether these are innate or learnt, but it is important that they can be inhibited.
    (f) Voluntary 'pain-terminating' behaviour – i.e., doing particular things in order to be rid of the pain.
    (g) Verbal behaviour of various sorts related to the pain: e.g., saying 'I am in pain' or 'that hurts' or 'that hurt frightfully'.
    (h) Various behavioural after-effects such as the avoidance of the pain-producing situation, together with other manifestations of fear, neurotic symptoms, etc.

This classification is crude and almost certainly not exhaustive; and well-known philosophical problems arise concerning the relation between some items (e.g., as to whether (c) is, or involves, a disposition to do (f)). But it is detailed enough to show how careful we have to be when we read in case-reports that, for example, after lobotomy a patient's whole reaction to pain was altered. In particular, it appears that, contrary to what we might expect, (e) and (f) do not always go together; some lobotomised patients have a tendency to wince and cry out more than before (possibly because the operation has diminished the inhibition against these reflexes), but their reactions classified under (f) and (h) are diminished.[1] Among the 'experiences' classified under (1), it seems fairly clear that those mentioned under (d) can be markedly reduced by lobotomy, although the patients say that the pain is as intense as before; and this would seem to apply also to those mentioned under (c). Patients who have had the operation are said to be no longer bothered or troubled by the pain of their disease; and they co-operate better with the surgeon even when he is doing painful things to them. It seems natural to suppose that if the reactions under (c) are reduced, so also are those under (b); and, if those under (b) are reduced, it is hard to deny that those under (a) are reduced too (how could I dislike the pain just as much as before, but have a smaller desire to be rid of it?).

But the descriptions in the literature are not easy for a philosopher to unravel, because 'pain' and similar words are used

[1] For references, see K. R. Hall, 'Studies of Cutaneous Pain', *Brit. J. Psychol.*, XLIV (1953) 289f.

indiscriminately by surgeons and patients, sometimes in the sense of 'pain$_1$' above, and sometimes in the sense of 'pain$_2$'. I am tempted to say that until some philosopher with a precise grasp of the distinctions involved actually has this operation done to him, it is unlikely that we shall be certain exactly what happens to the patient's dislike of the pain. For what it is worth, however, one surgeon says, 'In a sense, frontal lobotomy is not surgical treatment for the relief of pain, but rather surgical treatment for the relief of suffering'[1] and another says, 'Psychosurgery alters the subject's reaction to pain without materially changing his ability to feel pain'.[2] It is therefore not improbable that this operation can reduce suffering, distress and dislike without reducing the intensity of the pain-sensation. But whether it can or not, the suggestion that it can is a perfectly comprehensible one, and that is all that, as philosophers, we need. If we can understand what it would be for the suffering to be reduced while the sensation remained the same, we can surely understand also what it would be for the suffering or the distress or dislike to be altogether removed without any diminution in the pain-sensation. We may say, therefore, that the reports about this operation, obscure as they are, to some extent bear out the conclusions which we have already reached from examination of more normal experiences. We can also find in the reports examples of the conceptual difficulties which, if the word 'pain' has the two-faced character that I have claimed, we should expect.

Before leaving the subject of lobotomy, I will venture to make a tentative suggestion. One of the things that are most noticeable about these patients is that they in general stop being concerned about things; many of their other evaluations seem to go by the board or get reduced besides their dislike of pain. Thus one patient's son said of him, 'It would make no difference to Dad whether I told him I had won a thousand pounds, or that I was going outside to shoot myself'.[3] This, of course, entails a profound personality change, which has made surgeons very reluctant to use this operation except as a last resort. This lack of concern might be associated – I have not come across any

---

[1] Koskoff, in comment on Dynes and Poppen, *Am. Med. Ass. J.*, CXL (1949) 15 ff.

[2] W. Freeman and J. W. Watts, *Lancet* (1946) p. 955.

[3] M. Falconer, *Ass. Res. Nervous and Mental Disease*, XXVII 709.

clear evidence of this – with a shortening of the time-span over which the patient has fears or desires for the future. That could explain why patients who have had the operation to relieve a painful incurable disease cease to fear the onset of the attacks of pain. Now if the 'time-span of concern', as we may call it, were *sufficiently* shortened, would we be able to have any desires or concerns at all – since desire is always a desire for some future state (though this future state may be the continuance or discontinuance of a present state)? Is it not therefore logically possible for a patient to stop having any desires (to become quite apathetic, or in other words, not to like or dislike anything; for I cannot dislike something without, *pro tanto*, wanting it to stop, though of course I may want other things more)? But if so, is it not logically possible for him to retain his sensations, and in particular the sensation of pain, with undiminished intensity, while ceasing to have any affective attitudes towards them?

It may be asked whether there are any *drugs* which, as lobotomy has been said to do, could relieve suffering without diminishing the intensity of the pain-sensation. Pharmacologists evidently disagree about the answer to this question.[1] But it is certainly logically possible that such a drug should be invented; and we have in our common experience of alcohol something which comes near to what we are looking for. Before anaesthetics proper came into use, surgeons used to give their patients whisky before operations; as anybody may verify, this does not diminish substantially the intensity of the pain-sensation, but may make it a great deal easier to bear. In *King Lear*, Edmund says, as he slashes his arm (in this case, admittedly, for an ulterior purpose), 'I have seen drunkards do more than this in sport' (II, i); and it does not have to be assumed that the drunkards feel any less of the pain-sensation than sober men – only that they do not mind it so much.

6. It may be objected at this point that, if it were logically possible not to dislike pains, and therefore not to display the manifestations of dislike, such as withdrawal of limbs from the painful stimulus, children could never learn the use of the word 'pain'. For, it might be said, we can only learn these words because, when we are young, our elders see us displaying these

[1] For references, see H. K. Beecher, *Measurement of Subjective Responses* (1959).

manifestations, and say 'Does it hurt?', 'Have you got a pain?', etc. A philosopher might seek to prove thus that there is an analytic connection between having a pain and manifestations of dislike. But the argument is ineffective; for the teaching procedure would work perfectly well if the connection between pain and the manifestations of dislike were not analytic but contingent, provided that cases of pain without the manifestations, or vice versa, were rare. For me to succeed in teaching children the use of the word 'pain', it is sufficient for me correctly to *guess*, on one or two occasions, that they are in pain because they are doing what normally manifests dislike of pain; it is not necessary for me to be certain (let alone logically certain) that if they are doing these things they are in pain, or that if they were in pain they would be doing these things.

From the fact that certain contingent circumstances have in general to obtain before a certain word can come into use (even if this fact is itself logically demonstrable) it by no means follows that these same contingent circumstances are logical conditions of the word's correct use on a particular occasion, or determine what its *meaning* is on that or other occasions. Thus 'pain' might be the name of a completely private experience (a word which could be legitimately used whatever was happening overtly) even though the word could not have come into use unless, normally, these private experiences were correlated with overt occurrences. This point is of some methodological importance, but there is no time to pursue it.

7. In conclusion, let me satisfy the demands of honesty by declaring the axe which I have been grinding in this paper – though I fancy that its edge will have become visible to most people by now. There are those who seek to impugn the distinction between descriptive and evaluative judgements; and one of the arguments that I have heard used in this controversy is the following. To say that I am in intense pain is to state a fact; I cannot truly deny, if I have a certain distinct experience, that I am in intense pain. Therefore, it is claimed, the statement 'I am in intense pain' satisfies the conditions for being called 'descriptive'. But on the other hand, I cannot be in intense pain without thinking it bad, or disliking it, or suffering; to think something bad, however, or to dislike it, or to suffer because of it, is already to be making an evaluation. And (the argument

goes on) since all of this is true in virtue of the meaning of the word 'pain', 'I am in intense pain' seems also to satisfy the conditions for being called an evaluative judgement. Therefore, it is concluded, the distinction breaks down.

The answer that I would give to this argument will, I hope, be clear from the foregoing discussion. There may be a use of the word 'pain' such that it is analytic to say that a man who is in intense pain is suffering, or having something bad happen to him; or that a man who experiences pain always dislikes it. But if this is so, it may be only because 'pain' in this use is a complex word, implying *both* the existence of a certain distinct sensation, *and* suffering, etc. The argument does not rule out the possibility of a man having the very same experience except for the absence of the suffering. And if he did, there would be nothing to prevent him calling the experience which he had 'pain' in the sense of my 'pain$_1$', or, if this be objected to, using some other word. Let us, in order to avoid verbal dispute, use 'ϕ' for this other word.

Let it be admitted that, if a man is having the sensation ϕ, he cannot truly deny that he is having it. And let it be admitted, further, that if he is disliking the sensation, he cannot truly deny that he is disliking it (and similarly with suffering). This is the case, even if to dislike something is to make an evaluation; for if I am evaluating something in a certain way, I cannot truly deny that that is what I am doing. Let it be admitted, even, that on any particular occasion, if I do dislike the sensation ϕ, there is nothing I can do about it. This would not prevent disliking something from being a kind of evaluation; for there are many evaluations that are not psychologically *ad lib*. If I were flogged with a cat of nine tails, I should certainly dislike it, constituted as I am. But all this is not enough to establish the case of the philosophers whom I am now considering; for they want to make a logical, and not merely a psychological connexion, however inescapable, between experiencing the sensation ϕ and disliking it, suffering, etc.

If it be once allowed that, as I have been trying to establish, it is logically possible to have the sensation ϕ without disliking it, to have it intensely without suffering, and so on, the argument falls down. If I have the sensation called 'ϕ', all that I can be compelled logically to admit is that I have the sensation called 'ϕ'. Logic cannot make me suffer. That I shall nearly always suffer when I experience intensely the sensation called 'ϕ' is a well-established contingent truth. To try to make it more is to succumb to one of the oldest temptations in philosophy: the temptation to try to prove synthetic conclusions by logical considerations alone.

7 Wrongness and Harm

I am going in this paper to address myself to the question of the relation between my own ethical views, together with the theory of moral argument which I have tried to found upon them, and some apparently opposing ethical views which have been popular recently. It can hardly fail to strike anybody who reads the writings of the two sides in this dispute that there is much in common between them. I am referring not merely to canons of what counts as cogent philosophical argument, such as Oxford colleagues might be expected to share with each other but not, say, with a typical Indian philosopher of the old school; but, more specifically, to certain similarities between the contents of our views about the basis of morality, which keep on cropping up in spite of the apparent opposition between our ethical theories. This common element might be described as in a broad sense utilitarian, because all of us are founding our moral judgements upon the consequences, by way of good or harm to people's interests, that are likely to follow from alternative courses of action. This common element distinguishes both of the parties from those other philosophers who use the term 'consequentialist' as a pejorative label. Our ethical theories (that is, our views about the logical character and analysis of the moral concepts) seem at first sight very different; but the normative moral views to which they lead us appear to be in important respects similar.

What I have just been saying hardly needs illustration; but it may be of interest if I quote four passages, the first two from adjacent paragraphs of a paper by Mrs Foot, the third from Mr Warnock, and the fourth from myself.

> Bentham, for instance, may be right in saying that when used in conjunction with the principle of utility 'the words *ought* and *right* and *wrong*, and others of that stamp, have a meaning: when otherwise they have none'.

> I do not know what could be meant by saying that it was

someone's duty to do something unless there was an attempt to show why it mattered if this sort of thing was not done. How can questions such as 'What does it matter ?', 'what harm does it do ?', 'what advantage is there in . . . ?', 'why is it important ?', be set aside here ?

('Moral Arguments', *Mind*, LXVII (1958) 510)

It appears at least enormously plausible to say that one who professes to be making a moral judgement *must* at least profess that what is at issue is the good or harm, well-being or otherwise, of human beings – that what he regards as morally wrong is somehow damaging, and what he regards as morally right is somehow beneficial. There is no doubt at all that, apart from its high degree of vagueness, this would not be a sufficient characterisation of moral judgement; nevertheless it does appear to me to mention a feature which, in one way or another, any intelligible theory must recognise to be of central importance.

(*Contemporary Moral Philosophy*, pp. 57 f.)

The duties which we acknowledge towards people are not derived from the 'essence of man' or from any philosophical mystifications of that sort; they are acknowledged because we say 'There, but for my good fortune, go I. That man is like me in important respects; in particular, the same things as cause me to suffer cause him to suffer'.

(*Freedom and Reason*, p. 222)

These are none of them definitive statements of our several positions; the last passage in particular is insufficiently general (see p. 101 of this paper and p. 113 of *Freedom and Reason*); but it is evident, at any rate, that all three of us are prepared, in arguing for moral opinions, to base our arguments on the good or harm done to people by actions; and this makes us all, to that extent, utilitarians.[1]

This will appear paradoxical only to those who have not seen how the logic of moral argument works. The difference between

[1] Since this article was written, the development of Mrs Foot's and Mr Warnock's thought has proceeded on lines different from each other and from that which I had (too boldly) divined from passages such as I have quoted. The latter, in his latest book, *The Object of Morality* (1971), rejects utilitarianism, but still appears to want to make his moral views follow from his account of what morality *is* (see my forthcoming review in *Ratio*). The former, as it would seem from an unpublished paper which I have had the benefit of hearing, now wishes to reject morality itself.

the two parties is not that they espouse different theories of moral argument; it is rather that they espouse broadly similar theories, all of which lay stress on a conceptual connexion between wrongness and harm, but that one party has a less simple, and at the same time more fully worked out, idea of the nature of this connexion. The simpler theory looks as if it were designed to leap straight from the fact that a certain action would cause harm to people, via an alleged analytical connexion founded on a naturalistic account of the meanings of the moral words, to the conclusion that the action would be bad or wrong. The more developed theory gets from the same fact to the same conclusion by a more roundabout method of argument, set out much more fully, and founded on a non-naturalistic account of their meanings. The second party might therefore claim with some justice that it has really shown why, and in what way, such facts are reasons for moral judgements, by showing how the logical steps involved are rendered valid by the logical character of the moral concepts, and what other conditions have to be satisfied; and that it is only by a proper understanding of this that the cogency of the whole argument can be displayed.

In order to justify these polemical remarks, let us ask how a member of each party might seek to validate the judgement that an act would be wrong by appealing to the fact that it would cause harm to people (how, that is to say, he might try to bring someone who disputed it to admit that this really was a reason for saying that the act was wrong). Let us take the naturalist first (a straw man, admittedly, who cannot match the subtleties of real philosophers, but whose predicament will perhaps shed some light on them). We give him simply the premiss that the act would cause harm to people. Two weaknesses in his position will at once be apparent. The first is that no account has been given of the meaning or logical character of the premiss (of what we mean when we say that harm would be caused to people, and of what follows from this). In default of such an account, it is not going to be easy for the naturalist to tell us how his argument gets its force. I am not here alluding to a difficulty which has often been raised against utilitarians – the difficulty that the allegedly empirical facts upon which they say we should found our moral judgements, such as the fact that a certain action would minimise harm, are not really empirical facts at all, but value-judgements which we cannot get made unless we have some way of making value-judgements independent of the utilitarian way. This line of attack may indeed be open to the opponents of naturalisms of the sort I am dealing with; but I am not myself pursuing it, because I have *given* the naturalist his premiss. My difficulty is a different one: if we do not know what is the logical character of the premiss, how are we ever to know what follows logically from it?

The second weakness in the naturalist's position is a special case of the first. Not only has he not put us in a position to determine what follows from his premiss; he has claimed (or so it appears) that some things follow from it which certainly seem by no means to follow. For it does not seem to follow, from the fact that a certain act would cause harm to people, that it would be wrong. In default of an adequate account of the concepts used, how are we to defend ourselves against, for example, a retributivist who claims that harm positively *ought* to be done to the man who has done a wrong, and that the fact that this would be doing harm to a person (even though there is no compensating good to anybody else) is, so far from being a reason *against* doing it, a reason, in a case of this kind, *for* doing it? This objection can, of course, be answered – by someone who knows how the concepts work; but our naturalist's position will remain weak until he has explained this.

In general, how is the naturalist who relies on the notion of harm going to distinguish between the cases in which consequential harm is a sufficient reason for saying that an action would be wrong, and those in which it is not a sufficient reason? In answer to this too simple challenge, the naturalist will no doubt say that it *is* too simple, because it represents his own position as being simpler than it is. He is not saying that any and every consequential harm is a sufficient reason for calling an action wrong. He is saying only that it is *a* reason, which may be counterbalanced by other reasons, themselves also having the form of consequential harms, for calling all the possible alternative actions wrong; and that when he is faced with the choice between these actions, all of which are *pro tanto* wrong because of the harms which would result from them, he will judge that action to be, in sum, the right action which does, in sum, least harm. He will thus overtly embrace some form of that utilitarianism at which he only hinted before. I may not have hit on the precise form which he would embrace; there are many other possibilities, but I will not attempt to choose one or another of them on the naturalists' behalf, because it is up to them, severally, to do that. However, it is safe to say in general that one who starts off by seeking to derive wrongness naturalist-ically from consequential harm is going to escape from the sort of objection I have just mentioned only by embracing some form of utilitarianism. He will then say to the retributivist that retributivism misstates the moral reason for punishing people; unless the institution of punishment minimised harm to people, and unless the punishment of individual malefactors were necessary for the continued existence of this institution, their punishment, being in itself and considered by itself a harming of people, would be wrong.

So far so good. But the naturalist will now need to say how, precisely, this balancing of harm against harm is to be done. How, in particular, am I to balance harms to myself against harms to other people? The most obvious answer to this question that is open to our naturalist is the classical utilitarian one, 'Everybody to count as one and nobody as more than one'. This principle, however, requires a gloss. We need not saddle the naturalist with one out of the many possible views on the vexed question of distributive justice. Both sides in the present controversy are going to have trouble with that question, and indeed the same sort of trouble; I do not think that the differ-ence between naturalism and prescriptivism has any bearing on the matter – which is hardly surprising if, as I think, there is no substantial difference between the parties on *any* matter which is going to affect our actual moral arguments.

We may, however, with some confidence assume that, what-ever principle of distributive justice our naturalist adopts, it will be one which does not discriminate between individuals *qua* those individuals. We may assume, that is to say, that he will accept at least the formal principle of distributive justice, that nobody is entitled to privileges, or liable to be deprived of them, in virtue of being that individual, but only in virtue of the possession of some property or other which does not need references to individuals for its specification. I say this with assurance, not because *I* am a universalist (for I am not entitled to wish my own views on other people), but because *he* is a naturalist, and I have given adequate reasons elsewhere for holding that a naturalist cannot avoid being a universalist.[1] And Mr Warnock at any rate is one.[2]

Reverting for a moment to Bentham's principle 'Everybody to count as one and nobody as more than one', we may say that if this is interpreted in a purely formal way as merely banning principles of distributive justice which discriminate between individuals simply on the ground of their numerical difference from one another, both the naturalist and I are bound to accept it, whatever else we may wish to add. When I said that I was not going to saddle him with one out of the many possible principles of distributive justice, I meant that I was not going to commit him to anything more than this. And this, of course, is not very much, either for him or for me, by way of a solution to the problem of how, precisely, to balance against each other the various possible harms to various people that would be the consequences of alternative actions.

I do not think that either the naturalist or I can do without a deeper analysis of the notion of 'harm' itself. There seem to be some quite close conceptual connexions between this notion and certain others, which both the naturalist and I would be bound to accept, and which may be of help to us. To harm somebody is to act against his interests. What then are his interests? It is fairly obvious that the notion of interests is tied in some way or other to the notion of desires and that of wanting. Admittedly, it is not universally the case that if we want something, it is in our interest to have it, nor that if something is in our interest, we want it. I do not think that anyone would maintain so crude a connexion as this between the notions. But a connexion there surely is. In *Freedom and Reason* I expressed the connexion thus: 'to have an interest is for there to be something which one wants (or may want), or which is (or may be) a means, necessary or sufficient, for the attainment of something which one wants (or may want)' (p. 157). Earlier I used the expression 'is likely to' instead of 'may' (p. 122); I do not think that either formulation is entirely satisfactory, and probably something more complicated is required. But these complications need not concern us here. I hope it may be granted that there is some such connexion as this between the notions. That there is, is

[1] *Freedom and Reason*, p. 19.   [2] *Contemporary Moral Philosophy*, p. 43.

evident from the fact that it would be scarcely intelligible to claim that a certain thing was in a man's interest, although he neither wanted it, nor had ever wanted it, nor would ever want it, nor anything that it was a necessary or sufficient means to, nor might any of these things be the case.

I need to say something about the very general notion of *wanting* here employed. I intend it to be the equivalent of Aristotle's most general notion in this area, *oregesthai*, to be motivated towards the doing or having of. The noun corresponding to this verb is *orexis*, which is his most general word for 'desire', or 'being motivated towards'. It is, we might say, to be defined in a completely formal way: a man has an *orexis* to do or get or retain a certain thing if and only if, other things being equal, he will seek to do or get or retain it. *Orexis* thus includes what in *Freedom and Reason* I called 'ideals' (see p. 170 of that book). If we follow a policy which I am sure is the only one that can bring much clarity to this area, and insist always on giving the linguistic expression of these psychological states wherever possible, we shall say that to have an *orexis*, to want something, is to assent to a prescription of some sort, for example a universal or singular imperative.[1] If it is a desire to do something, the imperative will be self-addressed; if it is that someone else should do something, it may be addressed to him – as when I express the desire that the waiter should bring me some mustard by saying 'Please bring me some mustard'.

If there are, as I am sure there are, these conceptual links between interests and wanting, and between wanting and the assent to prescriptions, then the notion of harm, which in its turn is linked to interests, can be understood in the same terms. To speak very crudely and inexactly, to say that some act would harm somebody is to say that it would prevent some interest of his being satisfied; and this, in turn, is to say that it would, or might in possible circumstances, prevent some desire of his being realised. And if we are allowed to put this in linguistic terms, this is to say that there is some prescription to which he assents or might assent, whose fulfilment would be or might be prevented by the act in question.

This is too crude, because, if 'might' is taken in the sense of logical possibility, then on this analysis absolutely any act can

[1] See my article 'Wanting: Some Pitfalls', in *Agent, Action and Reason*, ed. R. Binkley, reprinted in my book *Practical Inferences* (esp. p. 51).

be called harmful; but it is hard to say how we ought to restrict the notion of 'might' so as to give the doctrine some content. I am not going in this paper even to explore these problems. I propose to assume for the sake of argument that there is some conceptual link between harm and the frustration of prescriptions which are, will or would be assented to. It is perhaps worth while digressing to point out that if there is this link, then only creatures which can assent to prescriptions can be harmed in the strict sense. This runs counter to our ordinary way of speaking. But I see no reason why the notion of harm, once established for creatures which can do this, should not be extended by analogy – and this in two ways. First of all, things like motor cars can be harmed when something is done to them which prevents their *users* from realising their prescriptions. This extension will be admissible in the case also of animals which are used, like horses, and of useful plants (e.g. apple trees, which we use to get apples from). But even where there is no question of a user outside the creature itself, there is a second way of extending the notion. We can speak analogically of the creature wanting things, and, as in the case of people, treat its goal-directed behaviour as evidence of this (provided that we also pay attention to the dangers in the analogy). And then it becomes only a pardonable artificiality to say that the creature is acting on what, if it could express them, would be expressed in the form of prescriptions. Aristotle, as is well known, extended the notion of wanting right into the inanimate world; he says at the beginning of the *Nicomachean Ethics* that the good is what *all things* desire.

It is only if we extend the notion of wanting in this way that we can reveal the origins of expressions like 'good roots' from which naturalists have drawn such sustenance; the apple tree's good roots, if they are not good for helping it produce the sort and the quantity of apples that *I* want, must be good for helping it to grow into the kind of apple tree that *it* wants to be – i.e. to achieve the *telos* or end of apple trees by putting on as perfectly as possible their *eidos* or form. If we had not inherited a great deal of this teleological language, we should not speak of good roots in the case of trees not serving a human purpose.

To return then to our argument: my imaginary naturalist opponent will not – or so it seems to me – be able to get much further with his project of showing the conceptual connexion between harmfulness and wrongness unless he makes use of the intermediate connexions which I have just been discussing, and in particular of that between wanting and prescriptions. In conjunction with the universalisability of propositions containing the word 'wrong' (to which, as I have already said, he is committed by his naturalism) this prescriptivist element in his doctrine, which has come in inescapably with his introduction of the word 'harm', does help him to do something that he and all of us want to do – namely, show how the fact that an action would harm other people gives us a reason for abstaining from it. But it helps him only if he travels very far from his naturalism in the direction of my own theory.

Let me clarify this if I can, by explaining in my own terms how I would accomplish the task which, up till now, I have been trying to help the naturalist accomplish in his terms of 'harm'. One might state my own view, summarily and formally, as follows: to say that an action would be wrong is to express a prohibition on it and on any similar action in similar circumstances. Now let us suppose that an action of mine would harm somebody else, and that nobody besides the two of us is affected. If the conceptual connexions which I have mentioned hold, then to say that it would harm him is to imply that the action would or might prevent the realisation of prescriptions which *he* does or will or might assent to. I should like to stress at this point that it is a *fact* that he does or will or might assent to these prescriptions; this is what gives colour to the claims of naturalists that the premisses about harm which they use are factual. And indeed they are factual, if interpreted in this way as statements about what prescriptions people do or would or might assent to. We shall have to attend carefully to this point when we come to ask whether the method of moral argument which I am proposing provides an example of an 'is'–'ought' derivation. It is very important that, although prescriptions are not statements of fact, there can be statements of fact to the effect that prescriptions are issued or assented to.

This action of mine, then, is going to prevent the fulfilment of the other man's potential or actual prescriptions. Why does, or why should, this lead me to say that it is wrong? In my own terms, why is the fact that *his* prescriptions would be frustrated a reason for *my* prohibiting the action and actions like it in

similar circumstances? It is a reason, because the similar circumstances include the hypothetical circumstances in which
I would be in precisely his position. Now *if* (and I stress the 'if')
I am seeking for universal prescriptions or prohibitions or permissions to guide people's conduct in circumstances like these,
I shall not be likely to accept a system of such prescriptions, etc.,
which does not contain a prohibition on such acts – acts which,
if I were in precisely his circumstances, including having the
same desires, would harm me (i.e. frustrate my prescriptions).

There are, however, ways of escaping from this argument.
At the cost of some oversimplification, they can be reduced
essentially to two, which were called in *Freedom and Reason*
'amoralism' and 'fanaticism'. The first consists in not admitting
any *universal* prescriptions, prohibitions or permissions for circumstances just like this (ibid., p. 101 (3)). The second consists in setting so much store by some prescription or other that
I am prepared to see it realised even if my other prescriptions, etc., in hypothetical or even actual circumstances, are
thereby frustrated (ibid., ch. 9). If I take neither of these two
lines, I am bound to assent to the prohibition on actions like
that which I was contemplating. And that is why the fact that it
would harm the other person is, for me, a reason for calling it
wrong. It must be noticed that (although the prohibition is
mine) the prescriptions (and therefore the desires) which are my
reasons for assenting to it are *his* prescriptions; and, as I said,
it is a fact that he does or would assent to them. It is also a truth
of logic that, if I were in a situation exactly similar to his, I
should have the very same desires, or assent to the very same
prescriptions, etc., as he does. If I did not, the situations would
not be exactly similar. So there is no further way of escape,
beside the two that I have just mentioned, which consists in
my saying that if I were in that situation, I should not mind the
act being done (ibid., p. 113).

This, then, is how I think the route lies from the factual
judgement that a certain act would harm another person to the
judgement that it would be wrong. Let us, by sticking to this
simple bilateral case, put aside the difficulties and complexities
that arise when there are many conflicting reasons involved,
some for saying that an act is wrong, and some for saying that
it is not; and let us ask whether we have here an example of an

'is'–'ought' derivation such as the naturalist claims is possible. Let us first notice that when I accept into my moral system a prohibition on the kind of act in question, on the ground that, if I did not, I should be failing to prohibit the frustration of prescriptions to which I would assent were I in this man's situation, I am not doing something that logic compels me to do. For it is not logically inconsistent to refrain from prohibiting actions which frustrate prescriptions which I will or would assent to at some time or imagined time other than the present. In general, I can without logical inconsistency prescribe the frustration of my own future or hypothetical prescriptions. A convert to atheism may prescribe that he be not given absolution on his deathbed, even if he then beseeches it. In such cases, there is some desire which the person now has (some prescription to which he now assents) by which he sets enough store to make him prescribe its fulfilment even though he knows that this may frustrate the fulfilment of desires or prescriptions which may be his in the future. And if we can do this even in the case of our own future desires, we can do it in the case of other people's desires. This is what lets in the fanatic.

There are, however, several different kinds of people who could be called 'fanatics'; and though I drew some distinctions in *Freedom and Reason*, it has become apparent that more are needed. I shall first mention a group of cases which fall short of true pure-blooded fanaticism, and then come to the true fanatic. This group comprises cases in which a man, for psychological, historical or other reasons, is unable or unwilling to do the kinds of thinking that are necessary before the logic of moral argument, as there described, will work for him. For example, he may pay no attention to the facts, or not try to ascertain them – either facts about how the experiences of other sentient beings will be affected, or facts of a more overtly observable sort. Or he may, because he is psychologically disturbed or unthinking or just obtuse, fail to make (or even to follow) the necessary logical moves. Or he may be using the words in such senses that these moves are not demanded. All these cases I allowed for in *Freedom and Reason*, and excluded them from the class of 'true' fanatics – i.e. from the class of those who, although they were using the words in the ordinary senses and paid attention to the facts and to logic, could not be touched by the method of argument that I was expounding.

We have to consider in particular, as a special case of these less than pure-blooded fanatics, the man in a state of what might be called 'universalised imprudence'. The name is appropriate, because, just as morality is a kind of universalised prudence (the man who thinks morally is consulting not his own interests only, but those of all equally), so this kind of fanatic extends his *im*prudence to his own and other people's interests alike. But the universalisation is, as we shall see, incomplete; for any sort of imprudence involves a failure to exclude indexical time-indicators (which are singular terms) from the maxim of one's action. The similarity between this kind of fanatic and the imprudent man is, however, illuminating. Just as the imprudent man is (often at any rate) one who attaches more weight to desires, pleasures, pains, etc., which he now has than to desires, etc., of the same intensity which he will or may have, so this kind of fanatic allows his present prescriptions to outweigh those to which he would assent, were he in the position in which he is now placing other people. For example, he now attaches so much importance to the prevention of miscegenation, that he is prepared to discount the sufferings that he and other people will or would have to undergo as a result of policies designed to prevent it. This kind of 'fanatic' does not have to have present desires which actually exceed in intensity the total of the desires of himself and others which the fulfilment of his present desires will or would frustrate; he has merely, present-ly, to attach exclusive or preponderant weight to his present desires or prescriptions, in the same sort of way as the imprudent man does. This, as we shall see, is what differentiates him from the 'true fanatic'.

The position could perhaps be stated with greater clarity if we were to translate the obscure phrase 'attach exclusive or preponderant weight' itself into terms of desires and thus of prescriptions assented to. Let us consider first the case of the imprudent man in the ordinary sense. He might be described as a man who lacks the present desire that his future and greater desires should be satisfied at the expense of his (other) present and lesser desires. The prudent man, by contrast, is the man who does not lack this desire; the intensity with which he now desires that his future desires should be satisfied is the same as the intensity of those future desires themselves; and if this intensity is greater than that of his other present desires, these latter will not be acted upon if to do so would frustrate the satisfaction of the future desires.

The troublesome phrase 'intensity of desire' can perhaps also be eliminated if we speak in terms of prescriptions. A desire is said to be more intense than another concurrent and conflicting desire if and only if it is the former that is acted on – i.e. if the person who has them and is faced with the choice between assenting to, and thus acting on, the prescription which expresses the former desire, and doing the same for the latter desire, chooses the former. It may be that this account is oversimplified; and it is certainly true that it does not cope with the problem of intertemporal comparisons between desires, let alone interpersonal ones. We have not, that is to say, explained how we are to compare the intensities of desires had at different times or by different people. But since that is an all too familiar problem which afflicts not only my own, but any utilitarian theory, I shall beg to be excused from dealing with it in this paper.

The imprudent man, then, is a man who now prescribes that the *fact* that he will or would assent to certain prescriptions in the future is not to be treated as a reason for assenting to, or for dissenting from, any present prescription. It is to be noted that in so prescribing, provided that he abjures the word 'ought' and such universalisable concepts, he is not guilty of any logical fault; for the fact that certain prescriptions will or would be assented to, or even that they are assented to, does not entail the prescriptions themselves. It is easy to be confused on this point.

The sort of 'fanatic' that I have been discussing is like this imprudent man, except that it is not merely his own future desires that he is disregarding in this way, but other people's (including their present ones); and this, as we have seen, is equivalent to saying that he is not now moved by the fact that he himself would have those same desires if he were in those other people's positions. We must now notice an important aspect of both these cases (already briefly referred to) which will enable us to simplify our account of fanaticism. Both these people are, in a similar way, failing to universalise their prescriptions. The key to understanding why this is so is to realise that the words 'now', 'present', 'future' and the like, which were used above, incorporate singular references to individual times. 'Now' means 'at *this* time', and 'future' means 'after *this* time'. The man, therefore, who gives a different weight to desires of the same intensity which he has at different times, just because the times are different, is differentiating between these desires on the score of a mere individual or numerical difference which may correspond to no relevant differentiation in quality – a difference which can be described only by bringing in singular references. It follows that he is not prepared to universalise the prescription to which he is assenting; it could not, therefore, be expressed by 'ought', or by any similar word. If the imprudent man tries to say 'I ought to satisfy my present desires but ought not to satisfy desires of the same intensity had by me in the future', he is open to the objection that, if the desires are of the same intensity, the merely temporal difference in the times of their occurrence cannot make a difference to whether he *ought* to satisfy them. There may of course be other differences, but to mention them would not be relevant to the case of the kind of (second-class) 'fanatic' now being discussed; for he is differentiating on temporal grounds only. It is perhaps worth while mentioning, in case anybody is in need of such a warning, that in all this discussion 'present' has to be taken as meaning 'present *now*' and not 'at any time present', and similarly for 'future'. For a person who had a principle of satisfying at *any* particular time *whatever* desires he had at that time would not be open to the objection just made.

It has become clear, therefore, that the kind of second-class 'fanatic' that I have been considering – the upholder of this kind of incompletely universalised imprudence, who is giving greater weight to his present prescriptions just because they are assented to *now* – is not a fanatic in the most pure-blooded sense. He needed to be mentioned in order to avoid confusing him with the fanatic proper, who, by contrast, does fully universalise his prescriptions, and can therefore express them with 'ought'. But, having been mentioned, he can be fairly easily put in his place, which is alongside the 'amoralist' whom we mentioned earlier. Both of them are people who fail to make proper 'ought'-judgements, i.e. judgements which they are prepared fully to universalise (over times and over people). We cannot have any moral argument with such people, because they are unwilling to make the kind of judgements of which such argument is constituted.

However, the existence of these two kinds of people, the 'amoralist' and the 'second-class fanatic', is sufficient proof already that the link between harm and wrongness which I have been trying to establish is not an 'is'–'ought' derivation. Either of these people, confronted with the *fact* that a proposed action of theirs would harm somebody else (i.e. that it would lead to something happening contrary to some prescription to which that other person does or would assent, and to which they themselves, therefore, would assent if they were in that other person's position), can reply 'So what?' Both of them can assent to the *singular* prescription 'Let it not be done to me if I am in that man's position' *and* to the *singular* prescription 'Let me do it to him now'. There is no way of logically compelling a man to make 'ought'-judgements; these people, who are prepared to acknowledge facts and to assent to singular prescriptions, but are not prepared fully to universalise these prescriptions, nor even to talk, in this context, the language in which alone this can be done, can always escape us. If, on the other hand, somebody is thinking morally about a given situation, and is therefore committed to prescribing, etc., universally, some action in all circumstances of the same kind, he is caught in the meshes of moral argument.

It is now time to turn our attention to the third, and only proper, kind of fanatic. He is the man who is prepared fully to universalise his prescriptions, and to speak in the language in which this is possible. He is not, like the 'second-class fanatic', differentiating between his own present prescriptions and his future or hypothetical ones, or other people's, simply on the ground that the former are present *now* to *him*. He gives his present desires priority, not on this score, but because of their greater intensity. When compared with desires for other things which he will or might have later, or with the desires of other people, these heroic desires of the true fanatic win, not because he fails fully to universalise and therefore gives *now* priority over *then*, but because they are so strong that they outweigh all the others. In some brief remarks at the end of my paper in *Jowett Papers* (ed. Khanbhai *et al.*), when I claimed to be able to show that fanatics must be exceedingly rare, it was this pure-blooded kind of fanatic that I had in mind.

I said there that such a fanatic, if he did exist, would pose a problem not only for me but for any kind of utilitarian. He is a man who has some desire whose intensity is such that, even when he gives equal weight to desires of equal intensity, no matter who has them or when, it still preponderates – and who is therefore prepared to universalise fully, over both people and times, the prescription which expresses this desire. In terms of the example of the Nazi used in *Freedom and Reason*, he is the man who so much wants there not to be people with hooked noses that this desire preponderates, even if he puts into the balance, at their full weight (just as if *he* were having them *now*), all the sufferings that the elimination of these people will cause. It is obvious that both the utilitarians and I will have to say that such a heroic desire, if it occurred, ought to be satisfied. The utilitarians will have to say it because, in their felicific calculus, the satisfaction of this desire has *ex hypothesi* a value greater than that of all the rest put together. I shall have to say it because, when I try to find a universal prescription to cover situations in which there is someone who has such a heroic desire, I am bound, when I think of myself in that man's position, to say to myself '*At all costs* I ought to avoid the suffering that I should have, were a desire of mine of that intensity to be frustrated'. Both the utilitarians and I, therefore, have reason to be thankful that such a person is exceedingly unlikely ever to exist.

Both of us, however, are likely to be in trouble if, although no single person has a desire of such strength, there is a large number of people whose desires, though not so great severally, add up in total to an intensity which is sufficient to outweigh all the other desires of themselves and other people. Let us suppose, in terms of the same example, that there are ten thousand Nazis, all of whom have a moderate, though no doubt regrettable, desire not to look at hooked noses. And let us suppose that there are only a thousand people with hooked noses. The actual figures are not important; but it is obviously possible to imagine a case in which the numbers involved, and the intensity of the respective desires, are such that satisfactions really would be maximised, harms minimised, etc., if those with hooked noses were painlessly exterminated.

This situation, too, is fortunately unlikely to occur; but it is easier to envisage, and to that extent more disturbing. If I may speak for myself, my confidence that real-life situations of this sort will not occur is based upon my factual beliefs about what the world, and the people in it, are like. I believe, that is to say, that as the intensity of the desire required is diminished to a plausible value, the number of fanatics required to compensate for the diminution of the intensity of their individual desires increases to an implausible value, so that the case, taken as a whole, remains implausible. But the case is sure to be used in argument by those of a deontological or anti-consequentialist bent who wish to make difficulties for the utilitarian. To such an argument, the utilitarian would be well advised not to offer logical objections, but rather to say that, if he really found himself in such a situation, he would endeavour to get the Nazis to change their desires. Actual Nazis, we may suppose, did not dislike hooked noses just for their own sakes, but because they thought, erroneously, that hooked noses were associated with all manner of other undesirable characteristics. If all the Nazis whose reasons for disliking hooked noses were of this sort were shown their error, and only those with a quasi-aesthetic dislike of hooked noses for their own sakes were left, I do not think that any further argument could be brought to bear upon them; but by the elimination of the others the example has become that much the less plausible. I do not see that anything can be done about this remnant of hooked-nose-haters except try, by psychological rather than logical means, to get them to overcome their distaste. However, I shall not pursue this point now, since my only purpose in introducing it was to show that the utilitarians and I are in the same boat.

We can now return to the question of whether the argument from harm to wrongness, which I have tried to restate, provides an example of an 'is'–'ought' derivation. My view is that it *would* provide one, but for the two escape-routes which we have mentioned. The first of these, which I called 'amoralism', has now been expanded to include one (second-grade) kind of 'fanaticism'. One who took either of these lines might, as we have seen, admit the *fact* that a certain action of theirs would harm somebody. But they cannot be brought by logic to admit that the action would be, *pro tanto*, wrong. The second escape-route (that taken by the pure-blooded fanatic) is of a different sort. It is made possible by the fact that in any situation in which we are involved, even merely to the extent of making moral judgements (which are prescriptions) about it, *we* are one of the parties whose desires have to be taken into account. Now if we were to take these desires (i.e. the *fact* that we assent to the prescriptions which express them) as a datum, it would be possible (save for the first escape-route just mentioned) to reason from this fact, along with facts about actual and hypothetical prescriptions of others, to a moral conclusion. But we cannot take our own desires and prescriptions as a fixed datum. This is seen most clearly in the case of the fanatic; but there is no logical bar to anybody becoming a fanatic. Since there is no logical limit to the intensity with which one may desire the realisation of a fanatical ideal, it is always possible so to weight the scales that it preponderates over the other desires with which it is matched. Fortunately this escape-route is, for others than pure-blooded fanatics, of no practical importance, since we cannot alter our desires at will. But this second escape-route, although by itself it is no bar to an 'is'–'ought' *derivation*, in a sense, prevents our speaking of the *demonstration* of moral conclusions, because one of the premisses depends on the desire of one of the parties to the argument.

These questions can only be treated very summarily here, and it is obvious that much more needs to be said about them. Perhaps they will not become clear until we have available an adequate deontic logic, in which the relations between the various steps in the arguments can be formally set out, and the concepts (especially the various kinds of permission) more fully clarified. The pitfalls are so many that it is very likely that in this article I have fallen into some. But I hope at least to have shown that there is much common ground between my own theory and that of some recent 'naturalists', and that the major difficulties in the subject are ones which face both parties.